THE CRYPTO TRADER

GLEN GOODMAN was an ITV news reporter who traded the markets for extra cash – until one day he realised he was a successful trader who did TV reporting for extra cash. He famously turned a £3,000 trade into £100,000 by betting there would be a financial crash in 2008, an experience he later recounted in *The Times*.

He worked as a business correspondent for BBC and ITV News, interviewing Theresa May, Boris Johnson and David Cameron among others.

With his growing trading income, Glen was able to leave his job in his 30s. When he started trading cryptocurrencies, his Facebook page 'The Shares Guy' (www.facebook.com/thesharesguy) became the biggest trading page in the world. He is now regularly interviewed by the media including the BBC, *Forbes* and LBC, and is a contributing expert on cryptocurrency at the London School of Economics.

www.glengoodman.com

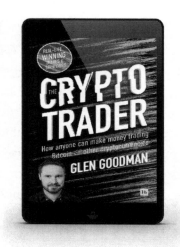

THE CRYPTO TRADER

TRADER

How anyone can make money trading
Bitcoin & other cryptocurrencies

GLEN GOODMAN

Hh

HARRIMAN HOUSE LTD
18 College Street
Petersfield
Hampshire
GU31 4AD
GREAT BRITAIN
Tel: +44 (0)1730 233870

Email: enquiries@harriman-house.com
Website: www.harriman-house.com

First published in Great Britain in 2019.
Copyright © Glen Goodman

The right of Glen Goodman to be identified as the author has been asserted in accordance
with the Copyright, Design and Patents Act 1988.

Paperback ISBN: 978-0-85719-717-7
eBook ISBN: 978-0-85719-718-4

British Library Cataloguing in Publication Data
A CIP catalogue record for this book can be obtained from the British Library.

CONTENTS

Preface   *vii*

Introduction: Crypto Riches   *1*

PART 1: WHAT'S IT ALL ABOUT?   **5**

Chapter 1: Cryptomania   *7*

Chapter 2: The Cryptoverse   *26*

Chapter 3: Mistakes, More Mistakes... and Turning
£3,000 into £100,000   *36*

PART 2: LET'S MAKE MONEY   **59**

Chapter 4: How to Buy and Sell Cryptocurrencies   *61*

Chapter 5: My Moneymaking Strategy   *84*

Chapter 6: How to Choose a Target   *96*

Chapter 7: The Clues are in the Charts   *104*

Chapter 8: Cryptofundamentals   *132*

Chapter 9: My Best Buys   *154*

Chapter 10: When to Sell   *169*

Chapter 11: How Much to Buy   *195*

Chapter 12: Short Selling   *203*

PART 3: PUTTING IT ALL TOGETHER   213

Chapter 13: The Missing Element   *215*

Chapter 14: Where's Your Head At?   *217*

Chapter 15: Escaping the Daily Grind   *232*

Chapter 16: And Finally...   *236*

Index   *239*

PREFACE

WHAT THIS BOOK IS <u>NOT</u> ABOUT

THIS BOOK IS not about how cryptocurrencies work and how their technology will change the world. If that's what you're after, just google 'How do cryptocurrencies work and how will their technology change the world?' It'll cost you nothing and tell you everything.*

WHAT THIS BOOK <u>IS</u> ABOUT

This book *is* about what you won't find for free on the Internet: the proven money-making strategies of a master crypto trader (that's me). So, what makes me a 'master' trader – do I have a master's in trading? Do I have my own apprentice? What I have is far more valuable: a track record of highly profitable crypto trading and nearly two decades of investing experience, first as a sideline, and then – when I'd made enough money to give up my day job – as a full-time occupation.

---

* Don't worry, I'll save you a google and explain the key points of the technological revolution in chapter 2.

When I say full-time, I don't mean full-time as in sitting glued to a screen all day popping stimulants. I mean full-time, as in going for nice walks with my wife, playing with my kids, playing with my wife, playing video games and sometimes trading. The kind of full-time that allows me to concentrate on writing a whole book about trading without harming my actual trading.

"Yeah, right!" you say. And so you should. If something sounds too good to be true, it usually is – especially in the crypto world, where scammers abound. You may be wondering:

1. *If this guy's strategies are so golden, why doesn't he keep them for himself?*

Well, my strategies are not my patented invention – they are the combined wisdom of many generations of master traders. I've read dozens of dusty books and thousands of articles. I've made countless mistakes and learned from each of them. Over the years, I've pulled together all these strands and have a successful technique I can call my own. I'm writing this book because I want to start a new trading revolution. For decades, most people have been handing their money over to wealthy, underperforming fund managers who cream off far too much of the pitiful profits for themselves. It's time for you to take back control of your money and your future. Hurrah!

2. *Yeah, OK, hurrah. But surely the more you spread these ideas around, the less of an edge you'll have in the crypto markets.*

My enemies are not the ordinary people reading this book. Even if ten million people copied my strategies, it would make no difference to my edge in the market because their financial firepower is too weak. My enemies are the professional banksters who already know all the tricks and use their vast financial power to manipulate markets and screw the little trader. Time for the little trader to screw back!

3. *But isn't all this a bit irresponsible? All the financial advisers in the media say we should put our money in a sensible tracker fund that copies the performance of the Dow Jones 30 or FTSE 100 index. You're just encouraging people to gamble!*

That is the precise opposite of the truth. It is actually the tracker fund narrative that's irresponsible, while I'm promoting more cautious yet also more profitable investing. Yes really. Let's say you'd followed the advice of the financial advisers and put your savings in a tracker fund in 2007 when they were all saying the banking problems would soon blow over. Over the next 18 months, you would have lost more than half of your life savings! Every trader has drawdowns* where they lose some of their profits, but if I ever had 50% drawdowns like that, I would pack it all in and pronounce myself a miserable failure. I've survived and thrived this long because I'm more careful than the supposedly cautious pension funds.

4. *But those drawdowns are fine because the stock market always recovers eventually.*

Yes… eventually. Though after the crash of 1929 it took 25 years to recover. It didn't rise at all between 1966 and 1982. And after the credit crunch, it took eight years for FTSE tracker funds just to get back up to where they had been in 2007. My trading technique generates higher profits with far less risk than a tracker fund. The fund management industry simply takes your money, gives you miserable returns and exposes you to enormous risk. Hurrah?

5. *OK, not hurrah, so I'll use one of those futuristic robo adviser apps instead.*

Knock yourself out. Just be aware that these simple algorithms stick your money in the same old tracker funds and charge you a tidy sum for doing so. The only difference between robo advisers and human ones is they can't physically grin while they're taking your money. Computer says no you can't have lovely big crypto gains.

---

* A drawdown is the percentage decline from the peak value of your investments.

6. *So where are all these so-called enormous crypto profits you keep boasting about?*

Here they are:

PAIR	BASE PRICE	P/L%
XRP/BTC	0.000037480	454.33
SAN/BTC	0.000087270	404.10
NEO/BTC	0.0027007	146.55
EOS/BTC	0.00027800	134.21
LTC/BTC	0.010477	50.41
BCH/BTC	0.11533	40.52
XMR/BTC	0.018739	32.81
DASH/BTC	0.055645	31.38
OMG/BTC	0.0011700	15.89
IOTA/BTC	0.00023700	13.74
EDO/BTC	0.00031490	10.23

POSITIONS (11)

One of my crypto trading accounts (late 2017)

That's a snapshot of one of my trading accounts in late 2017. The profits listed were made during a period of just a couple of months. Now those kinds of profits are not achievable every month, maybe not even every year. I had to watch patiently to seize the right moments to make those trades. But crucially, I achieved those returns without risking much of my trading capital. And even more crucially, I knew when to get out of the market with my profits, before the crash of 2018 took a firm hold. So how did I know it was time to take the money and run? All will be revealed later in the book.

7. *So it's all over now? The opportunity's gone?*

That's what the media say, so it must be true, right? 'Crypto is Finished', 'Bitcoin is Dead'. I'm happy for them to keep saying it. Every historic boom is followed by a historic bust, and it's only after the entire market is pronounced dead by the financial media and most investors have given up that the recovery can begin, leading us into the next boom. The cycle has repeated itself in every financial market since records began, but a relatively recent example is the dotcom boom and bust. Sky-high stock market prices for website start-ups led to a total wipeout in 2001–03. Fortunes were made and lost. Dotcoms were totally over, dude, and nobody wanted to invest in them anymore. Amazon's share price fell by an astonishing 94%, but behind the scenes, Jeff Bezos continued beavering away at his fledgling project regardless. Anybody who bought Amazon near the bottom, *after* that 94% collapse, would now be sitting on an eye-watering 30,000% profit.

Yeah, but Amazon had obvious potential back then, everyone knew that, but the financial experts say cryptocurrency is an overhyped technology, and the only way it might survive is if crypto companies combine with traditional banks.

It didn't look like that back in 2001, let me tell you. Here's what the *Economist*, for instance, had to say in March of that year:

> "Has the internet produced in the likes of Amazon… and eBay, a new generation of firms substantial enough to survive the bursting of the dotcom bubble? On their own, probably not. Hand-in-hand with an old-economy partner, maybe."

Ah. I take your point. So you think crypto has that kind of potential?

Yes, and I recently went on the record in a BBC interview, saying exactly that:

A ONCE-IN-A-GENERATION OPPORTUNITY

I've taken my years of trading experience and applied it to a brand-new market. Crypto is the Wild West of trading, and that means the risks as well as the rewards are greater. Even during the 2018 slump, I found there were still good profits to be made, though it's much easier making money during a raging bull market.

In this book, you will learn which sites and apps to use to trade cryptocurrencies. You will learn how to choose between the many hundreds of cryptocurrencies available, how to decide when to buy, how much money to invest in each crypto and when to sell.

This is a once-in-a-generation opportunity. I hope you grab it with both hands, as I have.

INTRODUCTION: CRYPTO RICHES

THE RISE OF the cryptos is one of the most extreme market events in *all* of human history. Yes, it's a very big deal. A multi-billion-dollar market has arisen from nothing in less than a decade. Huge fortunes have been made. Some, of course, have been made and then lost almost as quickly – as with any new market, there are dramatic ups and downs – but many more will be made in the future.

It's also remarkable because it's a people's revolution in the financial world. Nearly every other market innovation in history was pioneered by the big banks who scooped up the early profits and left only the scraps for the retail traders, the individual investors like you and me. This time, people like us are able to make big money while the banks sit around on the sidelines, frustrated and frightened by events they can't quite get their heads around.

Frankly, I've been having a wonderful time and now I'm inviting you to join me. My experience has taught me how to navigate speculative manias, weather the storms and come out on top. I'll pass all that knowledge on to you.

Here's a tip to kick off with. Joseph Kennedy – father of John F. – famously said he knew the 1929 stock market crash was about to begin when he started getting stock tips from a shoe-shine boy. My own 'shoe-shine moment' came in December 2017 when my mother-in-law asked me how she could buy Bitcoin. This stately lady had never so much as used a computer or logged on to the Internet in her life, but even she was now keen to hop on board the Bitcoin gravy train.

Now you could argue it didn't take a genius to work out that Bitcoin was overegged in late 2017. After all, TV news channels were wheeling out every pinstriped city figure they could find to solemnly proclaim that Bitcoin was a mere fanciful bubble waiting to burst, no different from the great 'tulipomania' of the 17th century.* But it's one thing to smugly predict a crash, quite another to get the timing right and make a lot of money. (Note: they did the former, I did the latter.)

I recount the wild story of cryptomania in chapter 1 and discuss how I successfully rode the ups and downs of the market. It's crucial to understand the stages of a speculative mania if you want to get rich from the next one. Because there most certainly will be a next one. And a next one and a next one and a next one. There always is.

In chapter 2, we go back to basics and find out what makes the cryptoverse tick. As I've already mentioned, this isn't a book about technology, but this chapter will provide you with the understanding you need in order to recognise any tasty-looking crypto opportunity that comes your way.

My own trading experience goes way way back to before the invention of Bitcoin (or the wheel), and in chapter 3 I recount some of the triumphs and tragedies – mostly tragedies – I went through while learning to trade. As you'll discover, through those big self-

---

* Tulips grown in the Netherlands had become very popular in Europe during the 17th century. A trend turned into a mass obsession and rare varieties of tulip bulb became insanely expensive in 1637, before prices suffered a spectacular crash.

inflicted screw-ups I learned some of the greatest lessons a trader can learn, lessons I will pass on without you having to go through the same pain... which hardly seems fair, now that I think about it.

Part 2 of this book is called 'Let's Make Money'. Woohoo. I'll show you the tools and tricks you'll need to become a successful crypto trader. We'll walk through the steps involved in opening accounts and executing trades, using price charts and researching cryptocurrencies. I'll reveal the crypto sites and apps I use to give me an edge over other traders. And all of that's just chapter 4. Chapters 5–12 are a deep dive into my trading techniques, how I decide what to buy, when to buy and when to sell, technical and fundamental analysis, going long versus going short, the essential skill of managing your risk level, and a fun chapter on my best buys.

In part 3, we'll put it all together into a cohesive trading plan. We'll also look at the common psychological pitfalls that trip up most traders and how you can learn to avoid them.

Once you've read all of that, I *defy* you not to become rich. Go on, try it if you dare, I bet you can't not become rich.*

---

* If richness fails, please turn your life off and on again until richness loads successfully.

PART 1:
WHAT'S IT ALL ABOUT?

CHAPTER 1: CRYPTOMANIA

"**S**O HOW MUCH exactly have you made? Enough to pay off your student loans? Enough to buy a house? Enough to never have to work again?"

The giant shabby hobo in front of me lumbered from foot to foot and grinned sheepishly.

"Um… never work again?"

Lars was a painfully shy Dutch post-grad student who'd started mining a ton of Bitcoin on his laptop when it was still worth just $3 a coin. Then he watched, bewildered, as the price rose to $100, $1,000, $10,000. What a jammy git! But I just couldn't bring myself to hate him. He was too damned lovable, even with all his undeserved riches.

"I guess I'll just travel around to some more of these blockchain conferences and have a few drinks and chat," he chuckled, handing me a business card which contained nothing but an email address: dx8j_-^+1+@7vt-8c-7np.com*

---

* To protect Lars' identity and his mountain of money, I have falsified one character in this email address. Good luck guessing which one.

THE CRYPTO REVOLUTION

I started trading Bitcoin in the aftermath of a big price collapse, but probably not the collapse you're thinking of. In 2013 excitement about this new funny money quickly turned to disgust as the world's biggest Bitcoin exchange, Mt. Gox, was hacked and 850,000 Bitcoins were stolen. The price of Bitcoin fell from a high of about $1,200 per coin to a low of $160, a fall of more than 85%. In 2014 I dipped my toe in the water for the first time, buying and selling around the $300 mark.

Now, if I'd had a crystal ball, I'd have held Bitcoin from that moment until the end of 2017 for a 6,000% profit and this book would be called *Cryptadamus: The Prophetic Bitcoin Billionaire*. There are probably a handful of cryptadamuses writing books right now. But the truth is, in the aftermath of the Mt. Gox robbery, putting more than a small chunk of your portfolio into Bitcoin was tantamount to handing over your life savings in exchange for a fistful of magic beans. The *Financial Times'* highly respected correspondent Izabella Kaminska wrote at the time:

> "We're going to stick our neck out at this stage and call this the end of Bitcoin."*

That was fair comment. There was a very real danger Bitcoin could collapse altogether or go on to become no more significant than E-gold. (Remember that one? No? Exactly.)

So, I was trading in and out of Bitcoin, making nice little profits for a while, but as crypto technology developed and improved, I realised cryptocurrencies were going to be the real deal. Steam engines, electricity, telephone, computers, the Internet, cryptocurrencies. This was going to be a once-in-a-generation paradigm shift from

---

* Izabella Kaminska, FT Alphaville, 19 September 2014 – 'Cult Markets: When the bubble bursts'. ftalphaville.ft.com/2014/09/19/1976132/cult-markets-when-the-bubble-bursts

old tech to new tech and there was no way I was going to stay on the sidelines and miss out.

WHAT IS A CRYPTOCURRENCY?

A cryptocurrency is a currency that only exists digitally. It has no physical notes or coins. You can usually only acquire it or spend it over the Internet, which involves transferring it from one account to another. There are over a thousand different cryptocurrencies, and some are worth a lot more per coin than others. Here are the prices of some of the major cryptos at the time of writing:

bitcoin	ethereum	litecoin
$5138	$159	$69

Back in 2014, all the talk was of Bitcoin one day becoming a major world currency, maybe even replacing the dollar as the world's reserve currency (the main currency used for international trade). My attitude was maybe it will, maybe it won't. However clever the technology was, world domination still felt to me like wishful thinking, a dream scenario for people annoyed about seemingly endless money-printing ('quantitative easing') by the world's main central banks.

But then came Ethereum. Far more than just a currency, it was designed to be a decentralised world computer. Suddenly the possibilities were endless: new apps could be written on top of Ethereum's code to solve countless world problems that had nothing to do with money. This invention completely blew my mind (man). It was my lightbulb moment.

WHEN LAMBO?

In 2017, the rest of the world caught on. Interest exploded and so did the prices. My Facebook page became a haven for hundreds of thousands of people desperate to know what was going on and how they too could grab a piece of the action, because everyone was saying Bitcoin's price was heading "To the moon!"

Newly minted crypto millionaires were spending their cash on fluorescent Lamborghinis to show off on Instagram. So now whenever a new crypto coin was launched (in what is called an **ICO** – or **initial coin offering**), all anyone wanted to know was how soon after buying some tokens would they be able to afford the car. "When Lambo?" went the popular cry.

Source: ilovecryptocoin.com

Unfortunately, as with all booms and manias throughout history, by the time most people got interested, the peak was already within sight. I cautioned my followers constantly that these were exciting but dangerous times, that if they insisted on buying Bitcoin they should only invest money they could afford to lose. Some listened, some didn't. The latter were generally focused on achieving huge, quick wins and there were plenty of unscrupulous con artists happy to sell them that false promise.

FOMO

In late 2017, my inbox was swamped with an unending stream of people demanding to know the secret to infinite riches. Telling them they'd probably already missed the Bitcoin boat just didn't cut it. The power of **FOMO** had taken a firm hold. FOMO is the acronym that launched a thousand memes. As you may already be aware, it stands for Fear Of Missing Out.

At least the memes proved there was a modicum of self-awareness among the people who were throwing all their money at $20,000 Bitcoin. They knew buying at what could be the peak of a mania might not have been the wisest move, but the fear of being the only one not to make it rich was too much to resist.

Many of these people were easy prey for scammers who promised large and certain profits if you just transferred $500 into their account right now...

Even those who had already been burned still seemed willing to give it another go. The guy who sent me this screenshot of his chat with a scammer had already been robbed of most of his life savings, but as you can see, he was sorely tempted to hand over his remaining money...

Source: Facebook.com

Swindlers started impersonating public figures. Martin Lewis of MoneySavingExpert.com complained to Facebook about all the scam ads using his name and face. I was even sent this friendly message by 'David Walliams':

David Walliams ▶ The Shares Guy. Bitcoin, cryptocurrencies & stocks.

59 mins · 🌐

I am a crypto trader and make over 200% a day, if you are interested,i can teach you trading or help you with the trading and turn $5,000 to $50,000 three months,please do note that cryptocurrency trading is not bitcoin but similar to forex,bitcoin it's traded for altcoins.also reach out to me if you are new to bitcoin and want to understand better,do not ignore this opportunity

Source: Facebook.com

If scammers can persuade you to buy some Bitcoin and send it to their Bitcoin address 'for investment', they can quickly spirit your money away through an untraceable series of transactions using ultra-private cryptocurrencies like Monero, making it virtually impossible to track them down.

WANTED: A SOLID, GENUINE PONZI SCHEME

If cryptocurrency was fertile territory for opportunists, it was also a breeding ground for highly organised Ponzi schemes.

Named after legendary swindler Charles Ponzi, these always involve persuading people to invest money in a scheme with the promise of unrealistically high returns. The organisers use the money from new investors to pay early investors the big profits they were promised, thus 'proving' to newcomers that they too can profit. The plan is usually to make the founders rich and leave the last (and biggest) group of investors empty-handed.

Charles Ponzi

OneCoin is an alleged Ponzi scheme with a modern crypto twist as it poses as a genuine cryptocurrency. Believing it to be the next Bitcoin, thousands of people around the world invested an estimated $2.4 billion* before its organisers in several countries were arrested.

I often warned my followers about OneCoin as well as Bitconnect, another highly popular and supremely dodgy 'coin'. You may have seen the viral videos of Bitconnect investor Carlos Matos whipping

---

* *South China Morning Post*, 29 May 2018, 'China prosecutes 98 people, recovers $268 million in OneCoin cryptocurrency investigation, report says'. www.scmp.com/tech/article/2148114/china-prosecutes-98-people-recovers-us268-million-onecoin-cryptocurrency

up a crowd at a rally in Thailand.* Carlos's infectious enthusiasm helped Bitconnect's 'digital tokens' reach an astonishing $3bn valuation in 2017. The scheme even had the seal of respectability of being listed on coinmarketcap.com, the leading cryptocurrency price comparison site, placing it in the world's top 20 largest cryptos.

Those of us who had learned to tell the wheat from the crypto chaff could see all the classic signs of a scam. The key warning signs to look out for were:

1. **Unrealistic claims.** Bitconnect promoters typically promised stellar returns of up to 40% per month. Ethereum's founder Vitalik Buterin said those promises meant it *must* be a Ponzi scheme.

2. **Multi-level marketing.** Bitconnect used the classic pyramid structure, paying existing members to recruit new members. This kind of affiliate networking structure is often used in legitimate

---

* www.youtube.com/watch?v=xK3yuxrmCac

businesses, but when it is used aggressively it can be a warning sign.

3. **Lack of transparency.** A key hallmark of most genuine cryptocurrencies is how open they are. The founders usually lay bare their programming code for other techie types to criticise and improve upon. They also publish a **white paper** with plenty of technical detail about how the system will work. Not only was most of Bitconnect's technology a closed book, but there was also considerable confusion about who actually ran the whole thing.

4. **Closed trading.** Genuine cryptocurrencies usually allow their tokens to be traded freely and openly on third-party exchanges, which allows buyers and sellers to determine the market price. Trading of Bitconnect's tokens was tightly controlled in-house for much of its lifespan.

In January 2018, law enforcement authorities closed in and Bitconnect shut down its exchange platform. The tokens went from a high of $475 to 41 cents each, a fall of 99.9%.

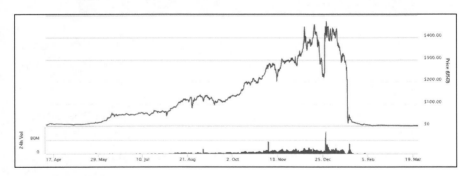

Bitconnect (BCC) price chart

Source: coinmarketcap.com

The promises were an illusion, but the victims were real. Social media was full of stories like this one:

> ## This cant be it. I lost everything. EVERYTHING
>
> This is all a bad joke right? It says BCC is at 30$ on CoinMarketCap. People on Telegram are telling me that BCC is not even 8$ worth now? If this is real, Im ruined. Like really f███ing ruined. I have nothing left. I put everything I had into this, because I trusted them. Literally all of my familys savings are in BCC, because a friend told me the risk was worth it. Are you telling me I lost everything? 80,000$ gone like nothing? Im so angry right now. My wife doesnt know yet. She will come home soon. What am I going to f███ing tell her. How am I supposed to care for my family now? I have literally nothing right now. My wife has two sons and I am unemployed. How am I supposed to take care of them now??? I hope someone pays for this mess. If not with money then with a sentence.

Source: Reddit.com

So, what happened to Bitconnect poster-boy Carlos Matos? He explained in a video that – like so many others – he had lost a lot of money in this "catastrophe" and felt cheated by "con artists and scammers". But he felt glad he'd been through the experience because of the valuable lessons it had taught him. Onwards and upwards, Carlos. Unfortunately, though, not everybody learns their lesson…

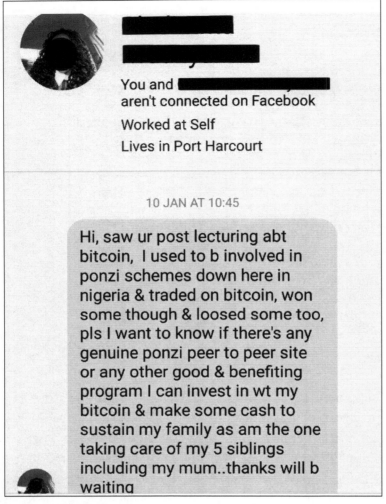

You and ████████████ aren't connected on Facebook

Worked at Self

Lives in Port Harcourt

10 JAN AT 10:45

Hi, saw ur post lecturing abt bitcoin, I used to b involved in ponzi schemes down here in nigeria & traded on bitcoin, won some though & loosed some too, pls I want to know if there's any genuine ponzi peer to peer site or any other good & benefiting program I can invest in wt my bitcoin & make some cash to sustain my family as am the one taking care of my 5 siblings including my mum..thanks will b waiting

Source: Facebook.com

The lady who contacted me here was after a "genuine" Ponzi scheme…as opposed to what?! I did my best to steer her away from dangerous investments but like so many people, she still feels if she gets in early enough, next time she could be one of the Ponzi winners instead of one of the suckers at the bottom of the pyramid. Unfortunately, desperation to break out of difficult living situations often drives people into the arms of scammers.

THE SILENCE OF THE LAMBOS

On Christmas Eve 2017, I gave my followers an early Christmas present by sounding the alarm over Bitcoin. The two-year-long upward trend was broken. The party was over.

The Shares Guy
Published by Glen Goodman [?] · December 24, 2017 · 🌐

In some of my videos, I talked about how Bitcoin's price was rising like a classic "exponential curve". This week the price broke down through that curve.

This is a warning sign. The risks of investing are now greater. The price may perhaps rise again, perhaps even higher than ever before, but that nice, smooth, predictable two-year-price-rise is over now and nobody can know where the price will go next.

Source: www.facebook.com/thesharesguy

I sold all my cryptocurrency holdings in December and January, but most people were still hanging on, hoping for a recovery. At this point, they were no longer investing, merely gambling. The slightest recovery in price would spawn confident proclamations that once again, Bitcoin was heading...

Source: Marcus Connor

The 'Bitcoin Roller Coaster' meme became an iconic symbol of the emotional roller coaster Bitcoin traders were on. Every time the price perked up a bit, you'd see that meme posted all over social media. It was truly viral, spread by excitement-carriers and infectious to anyone who dreamt of untold riches.

This was the denial phase of the crash. As the weeks wore on, the price kept teasing investors by rising a bit after each major decline, but those short rallies became less and less convincing. **FUD** had set in. In crypto-speak, FUD is the flipside of FOMO. (Sorry, but you're going to have to know this stuff if you want to trade crypto.) It stands for Fear, Uncertainty and Doubt. It spreads through scary rumours on social media and depresses prices. Google searches for the word FUD skyrocketed in January 2018.*

Source: iNeedThis.lol

HODL

By February 2018, Bitcoin's price had fallen from almost $20,000 to $6,000. Many people were still 'HODLing'. This ubiquitous term originated in a Bitcoin forum when a user (who admitted he was drunk) accidentally misspelt the word 'hold'. **HODL** took on a life of its own and eventually was used to mean Hold On for Dear

---

* trends.google.com/trends/explore?q=fud

Life, i.e. *never* sell your Bitcoins, however much they rise or fall in value.

The problem with this philosophy is Bitcoin's price fell by more than 80%, and most of the people who were nursing that loss had bought near the top. Many other cryptos fell by 90% or more. It's very easy to say "Just HODL" when things are going well.

But try telling that to this guy:

How do I cope with these terrifying losses? I bought literally at the peak in January.

SUPPORT

Serious question. I've been developing the shakes recently. It's midnight where I live and I just woke up with an insane anxiety attack and almost fell out of bed.

I put almost the entirety of my life savings into crypto in January. Almost 80k which I saved up after 6 years of working full time after college.

Everyone was talking about how we were early adopters, etc, and I honestly though I was going to be a millionaire in a year or less.

I immediately lost 25% within days of buying. "This is ok" I thought, I mean it might have been stupid to buy after such a strong spike in January.

But now, I have 6k left.

six. f█████ng. thousand. dollars.

What do I do?

Source: Reddit.com

We'll revisit this redditor's nightmare in chapter 3 and learn how to avoid it.

Even if you can afford to lose all the money you invest, it is important to protect yourself not just financially but emotionally too. Losing most of an investment is deeply depressing, and the experience often puts eager traders off for life. I'll help you learn to roll with the punches in chapter 14, but you should aim to be on the receiving end of occasional stinging jabs, not Tyson Fury knockouts.

We now know that between December 2017 and the following April, $30bn of Bitcoin was sold to new investors by Bitcoin **whales**.* A whale is one of the 1,000 or so people who own millions of dollars worth of Bitcoin. Whenever the price falls fast, people blame the whales for dumping a ton of Bitcoin on the market and forcing the price downwards. Analysis shows that was in fact genuinely happening from December 2017 onwards. The whales had finally stopped hodling and were unloading their Bitcoin (de-hodling?) into the hands of new unsuspecting hodlers who had decided to hodl at precisely the wrong time. (I'm sorry, I'll stop now.)

From January onwards, people were asking me when the market would recover, but the end of a long bull market is rarely a straightforward affair. It tends to take quite a while to shake out all the 'weak hands', the people who bought high and are holding on for a recovery. Eventually most of them give in and sell… once the price has truly reached rock bottom. Only then can the market begin a recovery, based on a bedrock of strong hands who don't sell easily and hold up the price.

The cycle was best illustrated by Canadian economist Jean-Paul Rodrigue:

---

* '"Bitcoin whales" control third of market with $37.5bn holdings', *Financial Times*, 9 June 2018
www.ft.com/content/c4b68aec-6b26-11e8-8cf3-0c230fa67aec

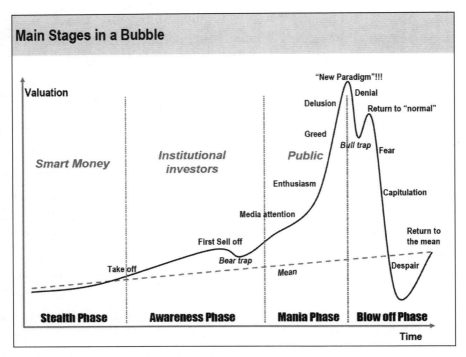

Main Stages in a Bubble

Source:Dr Jean-Paul Rodrigue, Dept of Economics and Geography, Hofstra University

So where did I sell my cryptos? At my favourite spot – just after the 'Return to "normal"' point. When the long upward price curve is broken I prefer to wait for confirmation of a truly broken trend (just in case it turns out to be a false alarm and the upward trend resumes). The confirmation occurs when the price rallies but fails to reach a new all-time-high before starting to fall again.

We'll return to this essential chart for a more detailed look in chapter 5.

By selling when the upward trend broke, I was able to collect my bumper profits and then sit tight, waiting patiently for the beginning of the next bull market. This may all sound very zen, but my ability to time optimal entry and exit from markets is the happy result of a long and painful trading education. By reading this book, you should be able to skip some of that pain as I took it on the chin for you. My trading lessons came the hard way, and some of yours will too, but by the end of this book you will know how to avoid the costliest mistakes and how to spot the greatest opportunities. You will be on your way to developing a trading edge to put you above the rest of the herd. So don't say I never give you anything.

CHAPTER 2:
THE CRYPTOVERSE

"[I like] simple businesses. If there's lots of technology, we won't understand it"

— WARREN BUFFETT, BILLIONAIRE INVESTOR, 1996

"We avoided the tech stocks ... our worst mistake in the tech field was [missing] Google ... we never owned a share of Amazon ... we missed it entirely ... I had no idea it had this potential ... I blew it."

— WARREN BUFFETT, 2017

"Cryptocurrencies will come to a bad ending ... [Bitcoin is] rat poison squared."

— WARREN BUFFETT, 2018

SATOSHI SPAWNED A MONSTER

IN JANUARY 2009 an anonymous coder calling himself 'Satoshi Nakamoto' created the world's first Bitcoin. Embedded in the computer code he wrote was the title of an article from *The Times* of London:

> "*The Times* 03/Jan/2009 Chancellor on brink of second bailout for banks"

This was a nod to Satoshi's mission statement. He was declaring war on traditional currency. He believed the global financial crisis of 2008 and its aftermath proved that national currencies needed to be replaced by something that could not be created at will by governments in infinite quantities and squandered by immoral bankers.

By 2009 everybody was already familiar with the idea of transferring money from buyer to seller over the Internet. Bitcoin was the logical next step – a new type of currency that had no physical form at all and existed only as computer code.

That is why you won't see any pictures of 'a Bitcoin' in this book (except for this one), because there's no such thing. That round thing you can see in the picture there? Doesn't exist.

Source: Pixabay/Creative Commons

By dispensing with notes, coins and any kind of central bank management, Satoshi's computer program allowed fast payments across international borders and low transaction fees.

Satoshi decided the number of Bitcoins would be strictly limited to 21 million, so they couldn't be endlessly issued and devalued like national currencies (which these days are **fiat currencies** – i.e. with no intrinsic value except what people agree them to be worth). New Bitcoins would be released into the system through a process known as **mining** and could be bought, sold and transferred to other people. Satoshi mined the first Bitcoins and set all the wheels in motion.

And then he disappeared.

He (she?) hasn't been heard from since, but Satoshi's Bitcoin addresses still contain about a million Bitcoins, untouched. In December 2017, these were worth over $19bn, making him the 44th richest person in the world.

In 2014 *Newsweek* sensationally revealed they had found Satoshi Nakamoto… except the poor guy swore blind it was a case of mistaken identity and attempted to sue the magazine.

Other people have since claimed to be the real Satoshi, but all their claims have turned out to be false. No doubt more wannabes will emerge in the future, but none will have credibility unless they can prove they possess the private keys to the Bitcoin addresses that hold Satoshi's billions.

MANIC MINER

To mine new Bitcoins, people use a computer program to solve a complex mathematical problem. Whichever miner solves it first adds a new **block** of recent Bitcoin transactions to the **blockchain**. The blockchain is simply a long list of all the Bitcoin buys, sells and transfers that have ever been carried out. The miners are rewarded for verifying these transactions with newly minted Bitcoins and transaction fees.

So far about 17m of the 21m Bitcoins have been mined. The rest will be produced gradually over the next century.

Mining was designed to get harder and harder. The days when people could mine Bitcoin on their laptop are long gone. The heavy lifting is now done by huge energy-guzzling server farms in countries where electricity is relatively cheap, but there are still opportunities for ordinary people to make money by mining other cryptocurrencies. People can buy very powerful bespoke PCs for a few thousand pounds each and mine less-well-known cryptos, hopefully to sell at a profit (after equipment and electricity costs).

BITCOIN AIN'T GOT NO BOSS

So what's the point of this Bitcoin thing anyway? If you want to buy stuff online, you can already use PayPal. Or Visa. Or Mastercard.

There is one key difference. Blockchain technology allows you to send money from person A to person or company B without the money going via any credit card firm, bank or payment provider. It cuts out the middleman. And that is one massively expensive middleman. Visa's revenues in 2017 were $18bn, Mastercard's $12.5bn, PayPal's were $13bn and American Express brought in $33bn.

The idea of Bitcoin is to have a single currency that can be spent anywhere in the world, so that people can send money to anyone anywhere swiftly and without currency exchange or other fees.

Nobody's in charge of Bitcoin because Satoshi's computer code runs the whole thing. It makes sure the transactions are verified by sending them around the network to be checked, it adds the transactions to the blockchain permanently, and copies of the blockchain exist on numerous computers all over the world, which makes it extremely difficult for anyone to hijack the core system. It's a truly *decentralised* database, an incredibly useful leap forward in technology. The dream of cutting out the middleman is powering the current explosion of ideas and inventions that will soon change our lives in many ways, some of which we can't yet imagine.

IMAGINEERING

Yes, I know my previous sentence sounds like some vague futurology nonsense. So put it this way instead. I go around speaking at cryptocurrency conferences and after my speeches, people come up to tell me about their crypto projects. Some of them are hopeless and ill-thought-out, but many of them are quite brilliant and backed by millions of pounds raised through crowdfunding and venture capital.

Had I been old enough to witness the explosion of ideas at early Internet conferences, I imagine it would have felt similar. While the authoritative voices in the establishment and the media at the time were pronouncing the Internet to be little more than an amusing conduit for emails, those in the know could see incredible possibilities.

Twenty years later, we all carry around Internet-enabled smartphones which have replaced home desktop PCs, camcorders, Walkmans, fax machines, maps, satnavs, newspapers, rolodexes, filofaxes, watches, Game Boys, torches, calculators, calendars, photo albums, encyclopaedias, dictionaries, dictaphones, alarm clocks, radios, notepads, answering machines, scanners, and – to a large degree – even books.

For an investor, unfortunately it's not simply a matter of buying a bunch of cryptocurrencies and waiting for the inevitable riches to arrive. When the Internet bubble went pop at the turn of the millennium, most of the promising young dotcom companies went bust, taking with them the savings of millions of investors. The same will happen to most cryptocurrencies, but a handful will become the Amazons and Googles of the future. Those are the ones you'll learn to profit from in this book.

THE EXPANDING CRYPTOVERSE

Imagine a taxi system similar to Uber but instead of paying around 20% to the company to run things, you just… don't. There is no company. Just an app that automatically matches up passengers with drivers, calculates prices and keeps a log of all journeys on a secure decentralised database, distributed around thousands of computers. The system runs itself. The cryptocurrency tokens you use to pay for your journeys serve as the oil in the machine, keeping everything running smoothly.

These taxi tokens may only serve this one single purpose. Our future may consist of a multi-crypto world where there are different cryptos for different functions. Rather like purchasing tokens to use for the rides at a theme park, you might purchase some tokens for taxi rides, different tokens for purchasing insurance, different tokens again for buying a house and so on. It sounds complicated, but all the token-exchange hassle would be handled automatically by the apps on your phone.

The result would be taxis without taxi firms, banks without bankers, contracts without lawyers, insurance policies without insurance companies and homeless shelters full of lawyers and bankers (only joking – or am I?).

That's what cryptocurrency is really about. People tend to get fixated on the *currency* bit and argue about whether Bitcoin will eventually defeat the dollar and take over as the world's main currency, but regardless of whether or not that happens, there are revolutions being planned in just about every industry you can think of.

The great opportunity for crypto traders is to find the apps that will become world-beaters and buy their coins/tokens at an early stage. If CryptoCabs* goes global then demand for its tokens would

---

* I just made that name up, but if you steal it and create a successful taxi app, then I demand royalties!

go through the roof, as many people would need to acquire them to pay for rides. As long as it's designed (like Bitcoin) to have a limited supply of tokens, each one is likely to become more and more valuable as demand goes up.

BITCOIN'S BABIES

The earliest cryptocurrencies were mainly **forks** or offshoots of Bitcoin (sometimes referred to as **altcoins**). The developers took Bitcoin's original computer code and attempted to make improvements.

- **Litecoin** – Debuting in 2011, Litecoin boasts faster transaction speed than Bitcoin. As late as March 2017, you could still buy it for less than $4. Nine months later it was nearly 100 times more expensive.

- **Dash** – Short for 'digital cash', Dash is a "decentralised autonomous organisation" which means changes can be made through a voting system by users. If you'd bought £1,000 worth of Dash when it was launched in early 2014, four years later your coins would have been worth £7.5m.

- **Dogecoin** – Invented as a joke currency with a cartoon dog logo, critics stopped laughing when the total value of Dogecoins reached $2bn in January 2018.

CRYPTO 2.0

If you want to find the next big money-making opportunities, crypto 2.0 is where the real action is. This giant leap from clever currency to world-transforming technology was the brainchild of… well, of a brainy child. Russian-Canadian uber-geek Vitalik Buterin argued that Bitcoin needed its own scripting language so that people could build useful apps on top of the existing code. He received short shrift from the Bitcoin community so set to work creating his own advanced cryptocurrency, **Ethereum**.

By the time he was 20 years old, he was the inventor of one of the most revolutionary technologies of the 21st century. So here's a message for school kids: don't be mean to classmates who look like this or they might not invite you to visit their private island when they become a billionaire.

Source: Romanpoet, Wikipedia Creative Commons

Ethereum is known as The World Computer. It is a decentralised operating system running on thousands of PCs with its own language which allows anyone to use it to create their own apps (or DApps as they're known). To run your own apps on Ethereum you have to pay using the native currency, Ether.

One of the main attractions is *trustlessness* – the system is not controlled by anyone, it's transparent, and strong cryptography means it's also secure (hence the *crypto* part of cryptocurrency). So, for example, DApps have been created which could count all the votes in an election. Anyone would be able to see the code used to count them, so there would be no way for corrupt officials to miscount on purpose.

Here are some of the most exciting DApps in development at the time of writing:

- *Augur* – "The Future of Forecasting". Augur will allow people to create markets and bet on anything. Initially it will be like a low-fee version of Betfair, allowing people to speculate on the outcomes of political and sporting events. Eventually, the hope is it will replace the world's multi-trillion-dollar financial derivatives markets!

- *Golem* – "Computing Power: Shared". Golem hopes to create a worldwide supercomputer by allowing people to share their unused processing power. All those PCs sitting around doing nothing will be harnessed and used, and their owners compensated with Golem tokens.

- *Etherisc* – "Decentralized Insurance". Life insurance, travel insurance, etc., all organised on a community basis and enforced using Ethereum's 'smart contracts' feature. No insurance company involved, so no need to pay the hefty fees of a big company.

- *CryptoKitties* – "Collect and breed digital cats". This is surely Ethereum's killer app, the use case that will send it mainstream. (Am I being sarcastic? I'm not sure.) Tamagotchis for the crypto age.

Source: CryptoKitties

ENOUGH TECH ALREADY. SHOW ME THE MONEY!

OK, you've got the basics now. The good news is you don't need to be an IT expert to trade crypto profitably. In this chapter, you've learned what makes cryptocurrency tick. We'll touch on the technology again from time to time throughout the book, but only when it helps us understand how to make money. Now let's talk trading.

CHAPTER 3: MISTAKES, MORE MISTAKES...

AND TURNING £3,000 INTO £100,000

THE GREATEST THING THAT EVER HAPPENED TO ME

WHAT WAS THE greatest thing that ever happened to me? My wedding? The birth of my children? No (sorry kids), it was losing all my money on a share called Gameplay in the dotcom market collapse of 2001.

How can that possibly be a good thing, let alone the best thing ever? Well, back then I was a naïve kid who got my first taste of trading – like most people do – through a 'hot tip'. My friend phoned me up (because we still phoned people up to tell them things in those days) and he told me I had to buy shares in the company he worked for. Gameplay were at the bleeding edge of the new online gaming industry and were already a stock market darling. He gave me a tour around their cavernous London offices. Two-hundred-and-fifty cool young trendies roller-skating around, playing ping-pong and tapping away on video consoles. These people were hipsters before there was a word for it. This was the future. I was blown away.

On my friend's advice, I bought my first ever shares with my £5,000 savings and saw them rocket in value to a high of £10.80 per share. This was easy money. I was making thousands! After five minutes in the markets I was already a trading genius. The evidence was clear; I had the magic touch.

Is some of this starting to sound familiar? If you spend much time on social media, you'll have come across noob traders – young men with a passable grasp of computer science who made a fast profit on a few cryptocurrencies and call themselves CryptoGuru or CryptoKing. If you want to know what happens to guys like that read on, for I, dear reader, was one once.

One fine day my friend called me up. Gameplay shares had halved in value... so this was an amazing opportunity to buy more of them at a bargain price! That's what my friend was doing, so there was no way I was going to miss out on the action. Sure enough, the price started climbing again. A couple of weeks later he called me up again. The shares had plummeted even further... so if we bought more at rock bottom, we'd really clean up, he said. I bought more. I was pretty much all-in with my meagre savings at this point, but the market didn't care, it just kept falling and falling, however much I pleaded with it to stop. Don't worry, my friend said, we can ride out the dotcom crash (as the newspapers had started calling it) and hold onto our shares until they finally achieve the stellar valuation they deserve. I was certain he was right.

And then he lost his job. Gameplay laid off nearly all their staff. Their idea was brilliant – nearly 20 years later online gaming is now a massive industry and Gameplay were there at the start – but ironically, they were too early, the Internet was still too slow, and they were spending too fast. Eventually the company was taken over and instead of being able to hold on until the shares recovered, I was forced to sell my shares.... for 1p each. I had successfully turned an investment of £5,000 into £10.

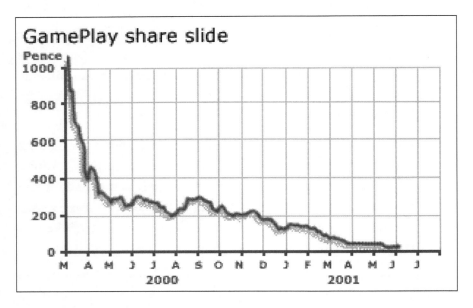

Source: ICV / Datastream

And that was the greatest thing that ever happened to me. Because for every pound Gameplay cost me, I have since made hundreds more from the lesson I learned. And that is the most crucial lesson in this book: ***never hold on to a losing trade.*** Ever. Ever ever ever. Don't rationalise it, don't try and justify it, just don't do it.

Follow that one single rule and you will dramatically improve your chances of trading success.

Preserving your trading capital is your **number-one priority** and that's equally true when you're trading cryptos. You may be lucky time and time again as you hold onto losing cryptos until they go back up, your losses are erased and you feel great.

But you need to ask yourself: *Am I trading so that I can feel clever or am I trading so I can make money?*

The answer to that question is crucial. If you are trading to feel clever, you will hold onto losing trades until they go back up and you don't have to face the painful humiliation of selling at a loss. That strategy will work some of the time, maybe even most of the time. But sometimes, your crypto won't go back up, it will continue down and down until it becomes the next Gameplay. A few losses on that scale will usually be enough to wipe out any gains you've made on other cryptos and severely reduce your capital, which will make it much harder to make decent profits in the future.

Selling a losing investment will crystallise your loss and that's a painful process. It means cutting ties with a crypto that you might have fallen in love with. You've learned all about it, you love the technology, you've taken the plunge, it's your baby... but it's losing you money! You have to cut it loose. Ultimately what matters is preserving the rest of your money for the next great trading opportunity, which will come along in five minutes' time. If you hold on to those losing cryptos until you've lost most/all of your capital, you're out of the game. There are no do-overs – as battle-scarred US trading veterans like to say.

Sorry, meme guy, I know if feels that way but it's an illusion. When the value of your crypto falls, that's real money you're losing. Your crypto is interchangeable with its current monetary value. You could sell it instantly for that number of dollars (or pounds or euros).

I would argue its monetary value is actually *more real* than the dollar/pound/euro value of your home. If a property agent tells you your home is 'worth' a certain amount, that may not be true. If you try to sell your home for that amount, you may or may not succeed, and by the time you actually achieve a sale, the market price could be very different from the figure the property agent gave you.

By contrast, if I tell you the crypto you own is currently worth $x, you could sell your crypto right now for almost exactly that number of dollars. So don't convince yourself it's just paper money or numbers on a screen. That's real money you're playing with. Never hold onto a losing trade – because that's your real money you're losing.

TO HODL OR NOT TO HODL?

But if I believe in a bright future for cryptocurrency, why don't I simply buy a ton of Bitcoin or Ethereum and HODL? Then I wouldn't even have to bother with all this trading hassle! There are a few good reasons why I don't HODL Bitcoin or any other cryptocurrency.

1. Brand names aren't everything

The idea that Bitcoin – the original and most famous cryptocurrency – may not conquer the world is blasphemy to some. I've stood on conference stages and suggested that very possibility to a chorus of gasps from crypto exchange owners whose very livelihoods depended on the success of Bitcoin. But nothing is guaranteed in this world and nobody can predict the future. In the 90s, nearly everybody using the Internet relied on an Internet browser called Netscape.

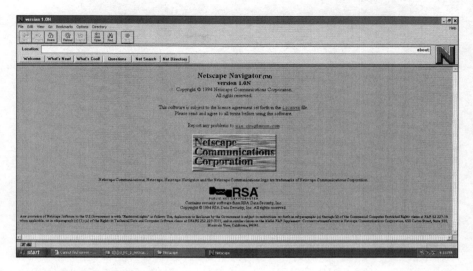

Browsing the web on Netscape

You can see from the picture that right from the start it had most of the essential functionality we take for granted today in a web browser. It was a household name. Its stock was worth billions of dollars. Surely that was a safe bet if anything was... until it wasn't anymore. It was beaten by Microsoft's Internet Explorer browser (which in turn was later decimated by Google Chrome). Netscape went from a 90% market share in the mid-1990s to a 1% share a decade later. The lesson is that a household brand name is a valuable thing but it does not make a brand bulletproof. Just ask Nokia. Or Blackberry. Or Kodak. Or Blockbuster. Or Toys 'R' Us. Or Woolworths.

Source: C. Ford, Wikipedia/Creative Commons

As for Bitcoin's future, it may indeed be exceptionally bright, but rivals like Ethereum or Ripple or a yet-to-be-invented cryptocurrency could potentially seize the blockchain throne, so for that reason alone I'm not prepared to simply plough in all my savings and HODL. The risk is simply too great.

2. Buffett's moat

Warren Buffett, the world's richest investor, ain't no tech genius, but one thing he does know about is successfully buying and holding: he's the undisputed champ. In some cases, he's held shares in a company for decades. He says, *"I don't want a business that's easy for competitors. I want a business with a moat around it with a very valuable castle in the middle."* What he means is that if he's going to make a long-term investment, he wants reassurance the asset is virtually impregnable. That usually means the company has a very loyal clientele who would incur a big hassle or cost if they switched their loyalty to a competitor. A lot of people own some Bitcoin now, but not many use it to actually buy things with (yet). It would be very easy for people to switch to one of its competitors (just as people switched from Netscape to Internet Explorer), so it's far from a sure thing as a long-term investment.

Some people see Ethereum as the ultimate HODL because thousands of apps have been created to run on its platform. An entire industry relies on the continuing existence of Ethereum. So is that a Buffett-worthy moat? Well... it's moat-ish. EOS is a rival cryptocurrency platform, and a lot of newer apps have been designed to run on EOS rather than Ethereum, so Ethereum's long-term future is by no means guaranteed.

Bottom line? Every major cryptocurrency has bitter rivals that threaten to be faster, more secure, more scalable. There's no sure thing in this infant industry.

3. Bitcoin has epic plunges

In 2011, Bitcoin's price fell by 93% and took about 20 months to get back to its previous peak.

In 2013, Bitcoin fell 91% and took more than three years to reach its previous peak.

Each one of those collapses was an opportunity to sell near the top and buy again near the bottom. Losing more than 90% of my investment every few years is not part of my personal game plan, so buying Bitcoin and holding it indefinitely is not for me. I'd rather profit from the uptrend and skip most of the nasty comedown.

CUT YOUR LOSSES

Most successful traders have a cast-iron rule that I think every novice trader should adopt. The rule is close losing trades and **cut your losses** while they're still small and inconsequential. Remember this guy?

How do I cope with these terrifying losses? I bought literally at the peak in January.

`SUPPORT`

Serious question. I've been developing the shakes recently. It's midnight where I live and I just woke up with an insane anxiety attack and almost fell out of bed.

I put almost the entirety of my life savings into crypto in January. Almost 80k which I saved up after 6 years of working full time after college.

Everyone was talking about how we were early adopters, etc, and I honestly though I was going to be a millionaire in a year or less.

I immediately lost 25% within days of buying. "This is ok" I thought, I mean it might have been stupid to buy after such a strong spike in January.

But now, I have 6k left.

six. f█████ng. thousand. dollars.

What do I do?

Source: Reddit.com

When I showed this post to a young trader I know, he said: "At this point he should HODL and hope for the recovery." I told him that's exactly what the poor guy would have been thinking when he had 60k remaining, when he had 40k remaining, when he had... you get the idea. Hope can be as dangerous to your account value as fear.

Also, if you lose 50% of your money on a trade, it's incredibly hard to earn that money back. Why? Because you have to make 100% profit just to get back to square one! (For example, if you have £100 and lose £50, you have to *double* your remaining 50 just to get back to your original 100.)

Still thinking you should hang onto those losers just in case they turn into winners? You don't need to take my word for it – there's plenty of empirical evidence to back up my rule. Check out *Performance of Technical Trading Rules* (Tharavanij, Siraprapasiri and Rajchamaha, 2015),* for example. These academics rigorously tested some of the most popular trading strategies over a 13-year period and concluded the main benefit of these strategies was not in identifying winning trades, but actually in making traders close their losing trades more quickly. In chapter 10 we'll look in more depth at how to decide exactly when to cut your losses.

As for me, I'd lost all my money on Gameplay but I'd caught the trading bug and was determined to learn from my mistakes. I spent the £10 I had left on a book about trading and my real education began.†

---

* www.ncbi.nlm.nih.gov/pmc/articles/PMC4583561

† OK, I didn't really spend that particular £10 note on my first trading book, but if this was a movie screenplay, then I'm pretty sure that's what would happen.

THE CLAN

"Aaaaaahhhhhrrrrrraggggghhhhh!" I screamed, as tears ran down my cheeks.

"That's it!" "Yes, man!" "Go for it! Let it all out!" shouted the other men in the church hall.

The sound that exited my body so forcefully was the primal expression of my frustration at a share falling and falling, my profit getting smaller and smaller, and then – as soon as I sold it – the market going straight back up again.

"Wraaaaghhh!!! Wraaaaaghhh!!!"

"Yes, dude, yes!"

The Clan* was possibly the highest-net-worth emotional support group in the world and I was the youngest, poorest member. This exclusive coven was the guilty secret of some of Canary Wharf's 'big swinging dicks'.† When the millionaire bankers and traders finished shouting into phones and punching the air for the day, they'd sneak down to an anonymous church hall, cry about how hard it all is and support each other's feelings. Seriously. I'm not making this stuff up.

Trading difficulties had led me to The Clan in the early 2000s. I'd read dozens of books and hundreds of articles about trading. I believed I knew what made a good trade, but I seemed to be sabotaging myself over and over again, breaking my own rules, throwing down the keyboard in frustration and repeatedly giving up, usually just in time to miss out on the perfect trade I'd been waiting for. I was desperate to find a solution.

---

* Please note, it's 'The Clan' not 'The Klan'. Ahem.

† In the 1980s, this is what successful traders sometimes called themselves. In *Liar's Poker*, Michael Lewis's classic Wall Street memoir, he says: "If he could make millions of dollars come out of those phones, he became that most revered of all species: a Big Swinging Dick… everyone wanted to be a Big Swinging Dick, even the women."

If you've traded before, you'll probably recognise this self-defeating pattern and may have suffered from it at some point. The greatest challenge for a trader is learning to understand your emotions, to listen to what they are telling you (as they sometimes contain useful gut warnings!) but not to allow them to dominate your trading.

And so, in a quiet little corner of the Internet, I found The Clan. They organised small gatherings of five or six top traders in church halls, mosques and temples all over the world. The first rule of The Clan is you do not talk about The Clan. Which is why I'm calling it The Clan (it's not really called The Clan).

Back in the church hall, before the primal screaming began, I was encouraged to open up about my frustration and, crucially, how it made me feel.

"Well I owned this share and it was my favourite because it'd been doing so well for so long. But then it started to fall, and I couldn't handle losing those profits. In my head, the profits were already mine, for keeps, but now they were slowly disappearing and I couldn't handle it, so I quickly sold to lock in my remaining profits. And as soon as I did the price went up again! Even higher than ever before!"

"So, dude, how did that make you feel?"

This was Scott, a hedge fund 'master of the universe'. Military academy, Harvard, Wall Street, Deptford church hall.

"It made me feel bad about myself."

"Yes but *where* did you feel it? Where in your body?" asked Hachiro (second place in the International Mathematical Olympiad, chess grandmaster, failing trader).

"Well, I had a sick feeling in my stomach. And butterflies."

"Right. Now concentrate on that feeling, concentrate on your stomach and express that feeling. Shout it out, bro!"

And so me and my gang of millionaires screamed our way to emotional health and better trading.

The mistake I was making was the exact opposite of the one I made with Gameplay, but equally devastating. Instead of holding on too long, I was selling too quickly. No share or cryptocurrency that rises in price will enjoy a smooth ride. It simply doesn't happen. Take Bitcoin. When you look at that nice smooth curve from 2016 to 2018 it looks like an easy ride (see figure 1). Who'd have trouble buying that and holding it all the way to the top?

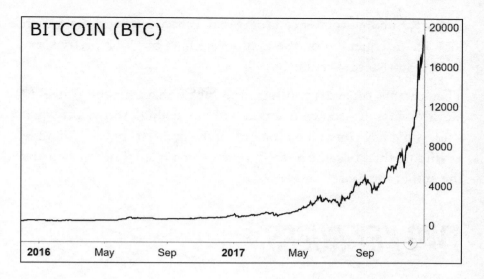

Figure 1

Chart by TradingView

But when we zoom into the chart, it takes on a very different complexion (figure 2).

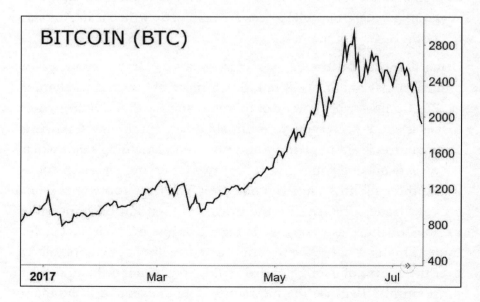

Figure 2

Chart by TradingView

In 2017, Bitcoin experienced some major price **corrections**[*] which look inconsequential on the long-term chart but look pretty scary on the short-term version.

That's a 30% price drop in June and July. It takes nerves of steel to sit through a drawdown like that without selling. And yet, if you'd sold, you'd have missed out on one of the greatest trades of all time, as Bitcoin then became a **ten-bagger** – rising ten times in value by the end of the year.

TWO KEY RULES

So now we have two key rules:

1. GROW YOUR PROFITS

2. CUT YOUR LOSSES

Sometimes they can feel contradictory. After all, I said I'd learned from Gameplay to sell my shares when they're falling, but now I'm suggesting *holding on* while prices are falling. So which is it? Answer: It's both. Bear with me here.

Being a successful trader over many years is largely about good money management. We'll talk much more about that in chapter 11. But for now, what you need to understand is that **cutting your losses** is about preserving your initial investment money. **Growing your profits** is about giving your trade some breathing space when it's *already* making you a profit. So, say your crypto has risen 100% in just three months since you bought it. You have 100% *open profit* on your trade. Chances are the price will then fall back, possibly by 30% or more as people start taking profits on their successful trade. This is a natural correction and usually happens regularly over the course of a long upward trend. So why not sell and collect those profits? Because the big money is in sticking with the main

---

[*]   A correction is a temporary decline during an upward trend.

trend. Take Bitcoin – simply holding it throughout the two-year bull market trend would have given you a 6,000% profit.

The real art comes in working out when it's just a temporary correction as opposed to when it's genuinely the end of the main bull run and the beginning of a crash. I'll help you learn to tell the difference in chapter 10.

WINNING!

With the help of The Clan, my trading performance was improving, but my big breakthrough year finally arrived in 2008.

I was still working as a business correspondent for ITV News, so I lived and breathed economics. Trading was still primarily a hobby, I wasn't earning enough to give up my day job, but that was about to change.

In 2007 we learned millions of poor Americans had been encouraged to take out mortgages they couldn't pay back. These dodgy loans were then parcelled up by banks and sold to other banks all over the world, which globalised the dodginess. When the penny finally dropped, banks became too scared to buy loans from each other, because they were unsure which loans were relatively safe and which were dodgy. British mortgage giant Northern Rock was in deep trouble, because it relied on these international loan markets to keep it going from day to day. There was a run on the bank with queues of people demanding to withdraw their savings from branches all over the country.

Source: Alex Gunningham, Wikipedia Creative Commons

So of course stock markets collapsed, right? No, they went up. Within two months, the US market had reached a new all-time-high. Every time I interviewed the CEO of a bank, they'd reassure me that everything was fine, the sub-prime loans fiasco was all being cleared up. I didn't buy it. They would smile shiftily while reassuring me (though bank bosses usually smile shiftily anyway). It seemed to me this crisis was too big to contain and was bound to get worse before it got better.

So what should a budding trader do? In his excellent book, *The Big Short* (which became a Hollywood blockbuster) author Michael Lewis tells the story of a handful of maverick hedge fund managers who defied the conventional wisdom by **shorting*** dodgy mortgages before other traders understood how bad these loans were. They made billions by getting it right, but *before* they were right they were very very wrong. Some of these guys were losing eye-watering sums on their short trades, as the markets continued to defy all logic and

---

*   Shorting is taking a bet that a share, currency, commodity or cryptocurrency will go down rather than up.

the market value of the bad mortgages went up and up – before *finally* collapsing.

Well done them. But that could very easily have been a story about maverick hedgies who tragically lost everything when they were forced to close their trades just before they were about to make billions.

As the great economist John Maynard Keynes said: *"The market can stay irrational longer than you can stay solvent."*

So to get around that problem, I watched the stock markets carefully, but I didn't start shorting the market until I was confident that it was really falling. As I later recounted in an article in *The Times*,[*] even with my precautions, this was still a scary time. The US market started falling and I was making money, but then it rose yet again until I'd lost all my profit, before finally the *true* collapse began and I really raked it in. Shorting is usually a tough business because the ups and downs along the way are that much more extreme than when you are trading the long side.[†]

The newspaper headline was *'My Little Short. How I risked it all to turn £3,000 into £100,000'*. When put like that, risking all of three grand to make a hundred sounds like a pretty good deal! Apart from the nice money, the experience gave me more confidence in my trading and I started taking it even more seriously, to the point where I was soon making more money each year from trading than I was from my TV reporting career. So I quit my job and never looked back.

---

[*]   www.glengoodman.com/times

[†]   I.e. when you are buying things and hoping they go up in price.

THIRD RULE: TRADE THE TREND

I buy into markets that are already going up and sell markets that are going down. Not every great trader sticks to buying things that are going up, some will do a lot of homework and buy what they believe to be a bargain, even while its price is still falling.

For a relatively inexperienced trader, that's a dangerous game. When you buy a cryptocurrency in a long downward trend, chances are it will carry on going down, at least for a little while, and you will be making a loss immediately.

Those *Big Short* guys traded against the trend, i.e. the prices of those mortgages were still going up when they went short, which put them in a very precarious position.

I find it safer to buy a crypto when it's already going up. Then you know very quickly if it's a good trade (because if it is, it will be making you money straight away!).

Some people find it psychologically very difficult to buy a crypto that's already going up because they feel it can't be a bargain anymore if it's no longer at rock bottom. It's important to acknowledge that a crypto can still be a bargain even if it has already risen a long way from the bottom. Bitcoin priced at $1,000 would seem expensive compared to when it was $100, but a few months later when it reached $20,000 that $1,000 would look like an incredible bargain. It all depends on your perspective.

Perhaps the strongest reason to buy cryptos when they're going up is the lack of solid fundamentals.* We'll get deeper into this in chapter 8, but the basic problem is it's very difficult to put a fundamental value on a cryptocurrency – what is it truly worth? Shares have revenues and profits which allow analysts to assign them a 'fair'

---

* Fundamentals are the underlying pieces of information that determine the true worth of an asset and its prospects for the future. Fundamentals of a company may include revenues, profits, assets, debts and cash flow. Fundamentals of a national currency may include interest rates, GDP growth and inflation.

value and decide whether the current price is too high or too low (in their view), whereas cryptocurrencies – particularly at this early stage of their development – are very much at the mercy of popular fashion.

Most cryptocurrencies benefit enormously from **network effects** which means they work more effectively if there are more people using them. So the more people buy them and spend them, the more useful they are in the real world and therefore the more they are truly worth. Likewise, as people lose interest and sell them, they become less useful and are worth less in a fundamental sense. So they are highly susceptible to becoming trapped in virtuous circles of growth or vicious spirals of decline. These strong trends are a nightmare for a fundamental trader, but a gift for a trend trader (like me).

SUMMARY: THREE RULES

1. GROW YOUR PROFITS
2. CUT YOUR LOSSES
3. TRADE THE TREND

If you've been interested in trading for a while, you've probably come across ads like this:

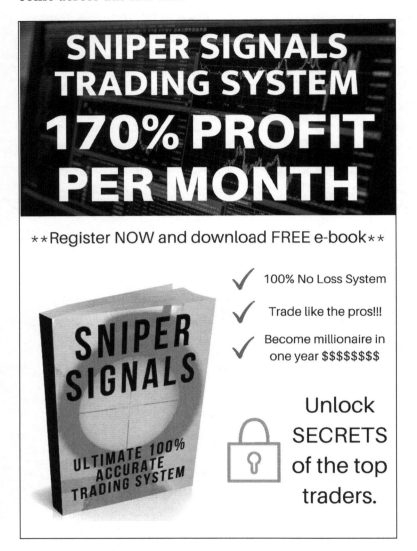

The profits promised by these secret trading systems are always lies. Forget 170% per month, let's pretend we're using a relatively low-powered 'system' that can make a mere 100% per year on average. If you start off with £10,000, after 20 years using that system you will have £10bn, making you one of the hundred richest people in the world. But what about all the people using the Sniper Signals system? I guess they must also be in the top 100 billionaires. Please excuse me while I lol.

In fact, only a few of the world's wealthiest people made their money trading. The richest trader in the world, Warren Buffett, has $84bn and his company has made about 20% per year for half a century. If you can make 20% per year consistently and keep reinvesting your profits, you'll end up wealthy too, due to the magic of **compounding.***

Let's say you start with £10,000, you make 20% a year trading and each year for the first ten years you add another £2,000 from your pay packet to beef up your trading stake. The results would be:

Start: £10,000

End of year 1: £14,000

End of year 2: £18,800

End of year 10: £113,834

End of year 20: £704,830

End of year 30: £4,364,121

Obviously, the more money you start with, the greater your gains. Stick a zero on the end of each of those numbers and you'll end up retiring on £40m, which will buy you a couple of hundred Lambos (assuming the ultimate goal is to spend all your money on Lambos).

The real secret is *there is no secret!* It's all about avoiding the mistakes most other traders make. See those three simple rules I wrote? Follow them with discipline and you will make big profits on trade after trade.

---

* Compounding is the process of continually reinvesting capital gains and interest on your investments which makes your wealth grow faster and faster, because each year you generate profit from your initial stake *and* from your accumulated earnings from earlier years.

In chapter 14 we'll look more closely at why most traders consistently make these fatal errors and usually never learn from those mistakes. These self-destructive habits are hardwired into our animal brains and we have to consciously unlearn them in order to become elite traders.

So is that all there is?

Nope, but you now have your solid trading foundation. With those rules in place, we're well on our way to helping you build an impressive cryptocurrency trading system to generate big profits. You may have some amazingly profitable years, as I did in 2017, but as we've seen, even just 20% growth a year on average would be enough to propel you into the wealthy elite.

PART 2:
LET'S MAKE MONEY

CHAPTER 4: HOW TO BUY AND SELL CRYPTOCURRENCIES

CRYPTOCURRENCY TRADING IS in its infancy, and trading platforms and exchanges are developing all the time, so some of the information in this chapter may become dated. But don't worry, I wouldn't leave you stranded with incomplete info, what kind of author do you think I am? On my website, www. glengoodman.com, you'll find up-to-date information about the trading platforms I use.*

This newness is a great thing for people like you and me because – as I explained in this book's introduction – something incredibly rare is occurring. In crypto, the little guys (with the right approach) are getting rich while the big banks and financial institutions have been left behind.

Cryptocurrencies were developed by computer geeks, a handful of these geeks got rich, and then the word spread beyond the geek

---

* Disclaimer: If you are reading this book in the year 2070 or later, I am now dead and sadly no longer able to update my website. Apologies for these foreseen circumstances.

community, to dorks, freaks and other assorted nerds. So they got rich too. Eventually men with trendy waxed beards and women who wear non-prescription Buddy Holly glasses got interested as well. But still no bankers. And that's because safe financial infrastructure for big investors takes a long time to develop and regulate. Bankers dealing with enormous sums of client money need to know it's definitely not going to get hacked and stolen.

The apps and platforms I will show you how to use were not designed for huge institutions – they were designed for regular folk, so we have the advantage. For now.

DON'T FORGET YOUR KEYS AND YOUR WALLET

When you sign up with an online platform to trade cryptocurrency, you need to transfer money into your account. Depositing fiat currencies like pounds, dollars or euros directly into your account often means paying big fees. Also, global banks have always been very nervous about dealing with crypto exchanges, so even the biggest exchanges have often struggled to accept credit cards and bank transfers on a permanent basis.* For these reasons, we crypto traders often prefer to first buy some Bitcoin with our own national currency from specialist Bitcoin sellers. We then transfer that Bitcoin into a cryptocurrency exchange and use it as our trading capital to buy other cryptos with.

When you buy Bitcoin through a website or app, you will create a **virtual wallet** to store it in. You will receive a **wallet address** and a **private key** to unlock that wallet. Both are simply long strings of

---

*   This situation is likely to change in the near future, so please read the very latest edition of *The Crypto Trader*. And if you're reading this after 2070 then please purchase the 50th anniversary gold edition, with a foreword by President Mark Zuckerberg explaining how the book changed his life.

letters and numbers that are unique to you. (Think of your wallet address as your personal bank account number.) If you intend to keep large amounts of Bitcoin in your wallet, it's not advisable to leave it in the wallet set up for you by the Bitcoin-selling website. However safe they promise their storage system is, you would still have to put your trust in the company. What if the company goes bust? What if the CEO runs off to the Seychelles with all your crypto coins? Will the government compensate you? Don't be silly. This is the unregulated crypto Wild West. You're on your own, cowboy.

Case in point: QuadrigaCX – a Canadian Bitcoin exchange – found itself in deep trouble in early 2019. Founder Gerald Cotton died suddenly and it seems only he had access to the passwords and recovery keys for the almost $200m of cryptocurrency in his care. At the time of writing, thousands of people are facing the prospect of never getting back the crypto holdings they entrusted to QuadrigaCX for safekeeping.

A safer option is to create your *own* private wallet, rather than trusting a company to look after it. Then you can decide how to keep your passwords safe and perhaps entrust a backup copy to a close family member.

Some types of Bitcoin wallet are more secure than others and usually there is a trade-off between security and convenience.

HOT WALLETS

Hot wallets are connected to the Internet. This means they are theoretically hackable, though the most reputable hot wallets are considered extremely difficult to hack. If you are only storing small amounts of Bitcoin, you may wish to take the risk for the sake of convenience. (Hint: I take the risk.)

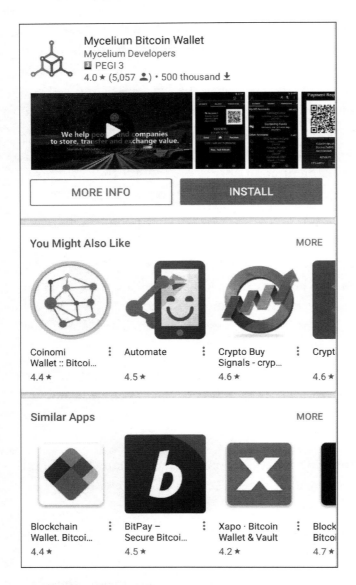

The Mycelium Bitcoin Wallet app on the Google Play store

One of the oldest and most popular hot wallets is the **Mycelium** wallet (no, they didn't pay me to say that, but yes, I wish they had). It costs nothing, so let's take a look at how to obtain it and review its functionality.

You simply install it on your phone (iPhone or Android) as you would with any other app.

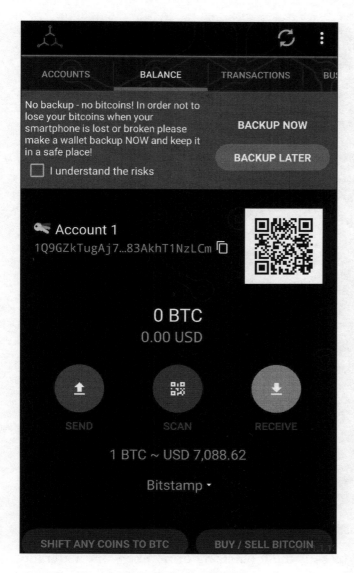

"No backup – no bitcoins!" So back 'em up...

The next step is to make a backup of your wallet, as subtly suggested by Mycelium's bright red *"No backup – no Bitcoins!"* warning. This backup will be a series of passwords you need to write down (using your physical hands and a writing implement) and keep somewhere safe.

An example Bitcoin address

The **Bitcoin address** is the long string of numbers and letters in the above screenshot. If anybody wants to send Bitcoins from their address to your address, all they have to do is type your address into their wallet app, or scan your QR code (the square pattern in the screenshot).

Feel free to experiment by sending as many Bitcoins as you like to my wallet address in the screenshot.*

---

* Sadly, I am unable (unwilling) to return any Bitcoins you send to this address. But please send them anyway.

Mycelium is very convenient – it sits on your phone, you can quickly send or receive Bitcoins from any other Bitcoin address in the world, so phone app wallets like this are a good solution for everyday transactions.

Once you send Bitcoins to an address, there is no way to undo that transaction. This is a key security feature of blockchains – it means nobody can steal back payments they've already made for a good or service. But of course that means if you make a mistake, your only option is to beg (or sue) the person who received your Bitcoins to transfer them back to you.

The Shares Guy
Published by Glen Goodman [?] · December 5, 2017 · ⊙

😰THIS IS THE MOST DESPERATE MAN IN THE WORLD!😰

James Howells from Wales had 7,500 Bitcoins on a hard drive which was put in the trash by accident in 2013. Those Bitcoins are now worth $80 MILLION!

The hard drive is buried deep in a huge landfill site in Wales, but James has offered to pay the local authorities 10% if they can help him find it. They have refused! He says they are crazy because they would get $8million if they help him.... See More

Sources: Facebook / James Howells

The flipside of having your own wallet and being in control of your own Bitcoins is that you are entirely responsible if you lose the private keys (and/or passwords) to your wallet. There's no higher power to call upon for a second chance. Just ask James Howells, an IT worker from Newport, Wales, who accidentally threw away the laptop containing his Bitcoins, which turned out to be a £100m error! (That was approximately how much his lost Bitcoins were worth at their peak price.) When I spoke to James recently, he told me he's still hoping to persuade the local council to help him dig up his laptop. He seems generally cheerful, considering.

COLD STORAGE

Mycelium is convenient but, because your phone is usually connected to the Internet, it's not somewhere you'd want to keep large amounts of Bitcoin. The safest options for long-term storage involve transferring your crypto into an offline (**cold**) wallet. If it's not connected to the Internet, then nobody can hack it. You can create your own paper wallet for free if you have a printer. It will look something like this one I just knocked up at Bitcoinpaperwallet.com.

An example of a cold wallet – on paper

You can see that it contains a Bitcoin address and a private key. Nobody can hack this scrap of paper... though it can be burned, lost, stolen, etc. The famous Winklevoss twins* were early Bitcoin

---

* Cameron and Tyler Winklevoss are best-known for suing Mark Zuckerberg because they believed he'd used their ideas in order to create Facebook.

investors and owned more than $1bn worth in 2017. They were so worried about losing their Bitcoins, they decided to cut the printouts of their private keys into pieces and then put each piece in a separate safety deposit box in a different part of the United States, so no thief could steal more than one piece of a private key, and of course you'd need the entire key to unlock their wallet.*

Clever... but inconvenient if you don't happen to be a billionaire. Another popular method is to store your wallet on a little USB drive or pay a bit of money for a special hardware wallet. Currently the market is dominated by these two devices: the **Trezor Wallet** and the **Ledger Nano S**.

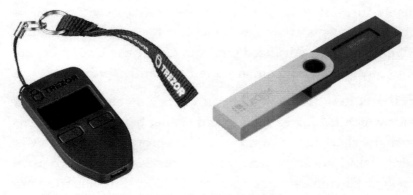

The Trezor Wallet (left) and the Ledger Nano S (right)

They're very safe and secure, you can even back them up with secret passwords which you can store elsewhere. But, of course, unless you carry them around with you everywhere, you won't be able to access your Bitcoins at short notice.

---

* 'How the Winklevoss Twins Found Vindication in a Bitcoin Fortune', *New York Times*, 19 December 2017.
www.nytimes.com/2017/12/19/technology/Bitcoin-winklevoss-twins

HOW TO BUY BITCOIN

If you're convinced Bitcoin's going to conquer the world and you just want to buy and hold a lot of Bitcoins, the simplest and safest way is to buy them directly from an established online platform using pounds, euros, dollars or another major fiat currency and store them in a cold wallet. In most cases you will be expected to upload photographs of your ID documents to the selling site/app to prove your identity. Some of the most popular Bitcoin sellers at the time of writing are:*

- **Coinbase** (www.coinbase.com) is regulated in the United States, available in most developed countries, easy to use on web or phone app, accepts credit cards, debit cards and bank transfers. By signing up to its advanced platform **Coinbase Pro**, users are able to buy and sell Bitcoin at more competitive prices.

- **LocalBitcoins** (www.localbitcoins.com) is a peer-to-peer service which facilitates buying and selling between individuals almost anywhere in the world. Users are protected by an escrow system – which means when a trade is started between two users, the seller's Bitcoins are put aside by the LocalBitcoins site until the payment has been safely received and only then are the Bitcoins released to the buyer.

- **Bitstamp** (www.bitstamp.net) was established in Europe in 2011, Bitstamp is one of the oldest and most reputable Bitcoin sellers. It accepts Visa and Mastercard credit cards.

- **Coinmama** (www.coinmama.com) operates in nearly every country in the world. Allows Visa/Mastercard credit and debit card purchases.

You can also buy other cryptocurrencies from some of these sellers, but for budding traders the problem with this method is you don't

---

*   Go to my website www.glengoodman.com for an up-to-date list of the most popular sellers.

get much choice. At the time of writing, Coinbase only sells five different cryptocurrencies (including Bitcoin), while one of the crypto exchanges in the next section allows you to choose between more than a hundred. When I'm trading actively, I don't want to be restricted to just five options. The greater the choice, the greater the opportunity to find a tiny crypto that turns into a big winner!

So I use my pounds to buy Bitcoins from a seller like those listed above and then transfer the Bitcoins into one of the exchanges listed below, to trade them for other cryptocurrencies.

CRYPTO EXCHANGES

At the time of writing, the most popular exchanges are quite new, lightly regulated at best and cannot be considered safe places to keep your money. I mitigate this risk in two main ways. Firstly, I use several different exchanges, so if one of them went bust, I'd only lose a small chunk of my capital rather than all of it. Secondly, I try to keep only as much trading capital in each exchange as strictly necessary. If I have surplus cryptocurrency, I withdraw it to a safe wallet or transfer it back into pounds.

I like to trade on the largest, most popular exchanges because they have greater liquidity.* More liquid markets tend to have much tighter spreads,† which greatly reduces your overall costs of trading. Make sure you check my website (www.glengoodman.com) to see what the largest exchanges are when you're ready to start trading. Let's review some of the top exchanges at the time of writing.

---

* Liquidity is the amount of buying and selling that goes on in a market, the amount of 'oil in the gears'.

† The spread is the difference between the price you can buy at and the price you can sell at. Tighter is better.

Binance

Founded in China, Binance (www.binance.com) is the largest cryptocurrency exchange in the world and allows you to trade a vast array of cryptocurrencies. It now has a base in Europe too. It charges relatively low fees compared to some of the other popular exchanges. Liquidity is high for the most popular cryptos, so spreads are relatively narrow. For example, if you could buy Bitcoin on Binance at $7,000 per coin, you could probably sell it again immediately for only a dollar or two less than that. On less liquid exchanges, that spread may be as much as $100, which means if you buy one Bitcoin at $7,000, you are immediately nursing a $100 loss, because you can only sell it again for $6,900. Spreads can make a big difference to your performance, particularly if you're placing trades frequently.

Binance's trading screen comes in basic and advanced variations, but there isn't much practical difference between the two. This is the basic version – it's bright and well laid-out:

The basic Binance trading screen

Source: Binance.com

If you're not familiar with advanced online trading, don't be freaked out by all the stuff going on in the picture. I'll walk you through all the important features of trading screens like this and it'll soon feel perfectly normal to fire up your browser and be greeted by a thousand flashing digits.

Coinbase Pro

Coinbase Pro is the advanced version of the popular Coinbase platform. Based in the US, it's well-regulated (at least compared to most other crypto exchanges) and has millions of users. At the time of writing, it still only offers a handful of cryptos to trade, but the options are expected to grow over time.

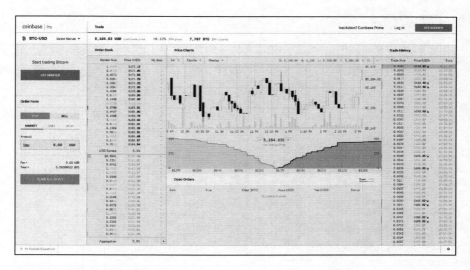

The Coinbase Pro trading screen

Source: pro.coinbase.com

Kraken

Established in 2011, Kraken is one of the oldest and largest crypto exchanges. It is also considered the exchange most secure from hackers, according to a report by cybersecurity firm Group-IB. It's based in the US, offers a reasonable selection of cryptos to trade, and is one of the few exchanges to allow leveraged trading on some cryptocurrencies.

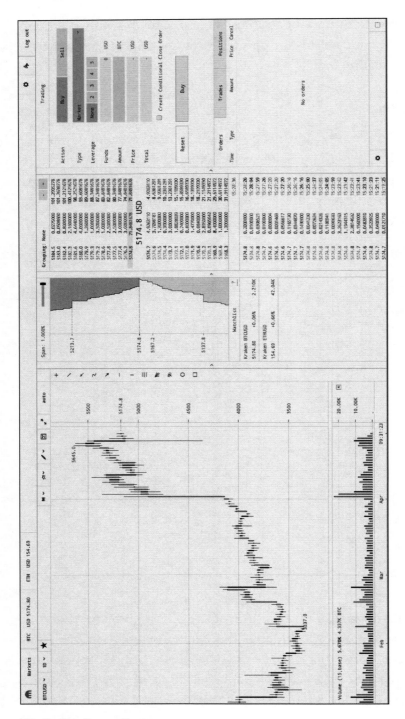

The Kraken Pro trading screen

Source: Kraken.com

Leveraged trading, sometimes called **margin trading**, means borrowing money to place bigger trades than your own capital would normally allow. It can mean bigger profits, but if not handled expertly it can quickly lead to big losses. I made a lot of use of leveraged trading during the 2017 crypto boom. By borrowing most of the money I was trading with, I was able to keep just a small percentage of my actual trading capital on any one exchange. This meant if the exchange went bust, there wouldn't be much of my real money in it to lose.

UNDERSTANDING A TRADING SCREEN

A trading screen contains several sections so let's review each of them separately. We'll use Kraken for this. If you're not familiar with trading terminology, this is the part of the book where you need to learn a bit of jargon. Take a little time to go through these short sections carefully to make sure you understand them. Believe me, it'll save you a lot of hassle later on if you get to grips with this stuff now.

Price chart

The chart can be configured to take up as much screen space as you like. You can use the built-in tools to add lines and annotations to the chart and use a variety of charting indicators. (We'll examine the features of a trading chart in more detail in chapter 7.) On the Kraken trading screen, the only indicator I've added is **volume**, which you can see along the bottom of the chart. The bars show the total value of all the trading that takes place in each time period (the longer the spikes, the more buying and selling is taking place).

Markets

If you click on **markets** at the top left of the screen, you'll see a list of all the cryptocurrencies available to be traded. They are listed by their three-letter codes, as you can see in the following screenshot.

All of these prices are in US dollars. The currencies are shown as trading pairs e.g. BTC USD is the price of Bitcoin in dollars, LTC USD is Litecoin in dollars, etc.

Asset	Pair	Price
฿ Bitcoin	BTC USD	5172.500000
Ł Litecoin	LTC USD	68.500000
◆ Ethereum	ETH USD	154.540000
◆ Ethereum Classic	ETC USD	5.445000
➤ Gnosis	GNO USD	15.010000
◊ EOS	EOS USD	4.561100
◬ Augur	REP USD	21.174000
ⓩ Zcash	ZEC USD	59.570000
ʍ Monero	XMR USD	60.800000
⊗ Stellar	XLM USD	0.096962
◂ϟ Ripple	XRP USD	0.291930
Ð Dash	DASH USD	107.596000
₮ Tether	USDT USD	0.976000
⦿ Bitcoin Cash	BCH USD	258.300000
◈ Cardano	ADA USD	0.068096

Markets

Source: Kraken.com

You can also trade BTC GBP or BTC EUR if you think BTC is likely to move more dramatically against the pound or the euro than against the dollar.

If you're feeling more adventurous you can trade other pairs, such as ETH BTC, which is Ethereum against Bitcoin. If you buy this pair, you will be betting that the price of Ethereum rises faster than the price of Bitcoin (or falls more slowly!). Trading cryptocurrency pairs allows you to take bets on the relative movements of each crypto.

By clicking on 'Bitcoin', I make BTC USD appear in the chart window and BTC USD come up on the trading form on the right of the screen.

Trading form

The **trading form** is where you place an order to open a new trade.

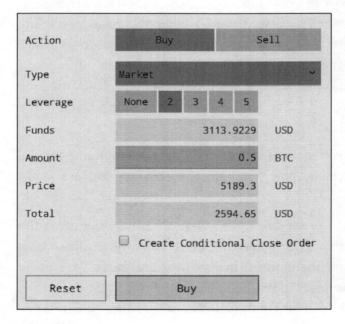

Trading form

Source: Kraken.com

You enter the amount of the selected crypto you would like to buy or sell. The dropdown menu is set to 'Market' which means if you click on 'Buy' you will immediately buy – at the current market price – as much BTC as you have specified in the 'Amount' box. In this example, we are buying half a Bitcoin. You need to make sure you have enough fiat currency in the 'Funds' box to make your purchase. Here, the price of 1 BTC is 5189.30 US dollars, so there are more than enough funds available to buy 0.5 BTC.

If leverage is set to 'None' then you are simply swapping some of your dollars for some Bitcoin. Conversely, if you already own some Bitcoin and you'd like to swap it into dollars, you click on the 'Sell' button in the trading window instead of the 'Buy' button.

If you set **leverage** to 2 or higher, then you can open a position worth 2×, 3×, 4× or 5× your existing funds, using borrowed money. This way you can buy up to 2.5 Bitcoins, even if you only have enough funds for 0.5 Bitcoin. But, of course, this is not a permanent purchase because that borrowed money has to be paid back some time, so it will register as an open position in the **positions** window. The hope is that the value of BTC will rise in the meantime and, when you eventually close the position, you will have made a profit on the entire 2.5 BTC you borrowed. And that's trading in a nutshell!

There are several other order types in the dropdown menu, as well as 'Market'. The basic types you need to understand are 'Stop' order and 'Limit' order.

A **stop order** is an order to buy BTC at a higher price than the current market price. You specify the price you'd like to buy at in the 'Price' box (and the amount in the 'Amount' box). Your order will not be filled unless the market price rises to that level. Instead, it will sit inside the 'Orders' tab (see the full trading screen a few pages back) and you can cancel your pending order at any time.

A **limit order** is an order to buy BTC at a lower price than the current market price. Again, you specify the price you'd like to buy at, and your order will only be filled if the market price drops to the level of your limit order.

Remember, if you're going short, those instructions are reversed. So if you want to go short at a price lower than the current market price, you place a stop order. If you want to go short at a higher price than the current market price, you place a limit order.

Confused? Excellent. Now you're a real trader!

Positions

If you open the 'Positions' tab, you'll see any trades that you've opened. In the example below, we have an open long position of 0.5 BTC, bought at $5186.70 per unit of BTC (so the total purchase cost was 0.5 × 5186.7 = $2593.35).

Orders	Trades		Positions
Side	Amount	Price	P/L
Long	0.5000000	5186.7	+0.01%

Positions tab

Source: Kraken.com

Under **P/L** you can see the position I've just opened has a 0.01% open profit. As the position was opened using leverage, you have to pay a small amount of interest on the borrowed money every day that it remains open. If you click on the position, a window opens giving you the option to close the position and return the borrowed money. The profit (or loss) you've made then gets added to your funds.

Order book

The **order book** contains all the Bitcoin limit orders that are waiting to be filled. If any trader on Kraken places a limit order, it sits on the communal order book until somebody else's order matches that limit order and one person buys from the other. In the example in the next screenshot, if someone places a limit order to buy BTC at a price of $5184.9, it will sit in the bottom half of the window. If somebody places a limit order to sell BTC at a price of $5185.6 it will sit in the top half.

All the other prices you can see represent all the other limit orders that people have placed at less competitive prices. If anybody wants to place a market order to immediately buy Bitcoin, they will be matched with a person who placed a limit order at $5185.6, as that is the cheapest price anyone is currently willing to sell at.

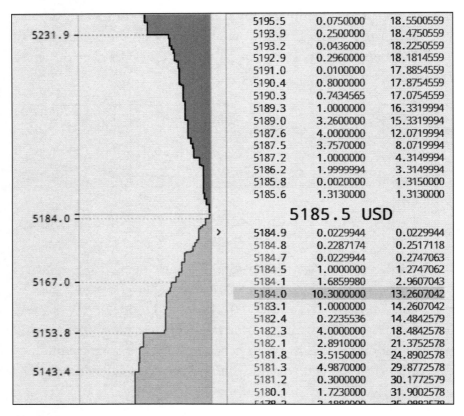

Order book

Source: Kraken.com

Because $5184.90 and $5185.60 are the best prices available to buy and sell at, they are considered the main quoted prices for Bitcoin and are called the **bid** and **ask** prices respectively. (Sometimes people use the word *offer* instead of ask.) The difference between the two prices is called the **spread**, as I mentioned earlier. Because Kraken has a lot of users and therefore a lot of liquidity, competition between all the traders tends to push the best buy and sell prices closer and closer together, resulting in a small spread, which in this case is less than a dollar. I'll stress again: this is very important, as a big spread can greatly add to your costs of trading.

You can see the *depth* of the order book by looking at the numbers in the middle column. They show the total size of all the limit orders placed at each price level. (Running totals are shown in the column on the right, and pictorially in the chart on the left.) For example, a total of 10.3 Bitcoins has been ordered to be purchased if the price falls to $5184.0. If that price is never reached (because there are better prices available to sellers) then those orders will continue to sit on the order book until the traders who placed them cancel them.

Fees

For most traders, Kraken currently charges a fee of 0.16% of the value of your position if you place a limit order. It charges 0.26% of your trade value if you place a market or stop order. This is because limit orders add to the liquidity on the order book, so Kraken encourages them with cheaper trading fees. Market and stop orders remove liquidity because they are matched with limit orders on the order book, and once those trades go through, the limit orders are removed from the book.

As I mentioned, if you are trading 'on margin' you will be borrowing – through the exchange – most of the money you trade with. You will incur interest payments for this, and you should always check what the current rates are in the **Support** section of the site.

SPREAD BETTING

If – like me – you live in the UK, then you're lucky enough to enjoy access to spread betting platforms, which allow you to trade with all profits completely tax-free!

Many of these platforms now allow you to bet on the prices of major cryptocurrencies. You are not actually buying and selling the cryptos themselves, merely betting on their price movements, but from a practical point of view the process is very similar. The platforms look and feel a lot like actual crypto exchanges, trading works in much the same way... except that all profits are tax-free!

They are currently very limited in terms of the selection of cryptos they offer, but there are some big advantages to using these platforms and I've made a lot of use of them to trade Bitcoin in recent years.

Apart from being completely tax-free (did I mention that?) they are regulated in the UK so your money is protected to some degree. Clients' money is separated from the company's own money and held in separate bank accounts so if the company is in financial trouble, clients' money is – in theory – unaffected. If the spread betting company has stolen all the clients' money before going bust then UK investors are eligible for compensation of up to £50,000 under the Financial Services Compensation Scheme.

At the time of writing the spreads offered on Bitcoin and other cryptos are far wider than the spreads on crypto exchanges like Kraken, so you will pay a big upfront premium for each trade in terms of the large spread between the buy and sell prices. But on the other hand, there is often no trading fee for spread betting (while Kraken, Binance and other international exchanges tend to charge fees).

Spread betting trades are often leveraged, so you will also pay an interest rate to borrow most of the money for going long on cryptos. The interest rate tends to be about 2.5% or 3% above the

Bank of England base rate. At the time of writing, the base rate is 0.75%, so leveraged bets are usually charged at about 3.25% per year. If you open a leveraged bet on Bitcoin and keep it open for three months, you'll pay 3.25 ÷ 4 = 0.8125% interest on the loaned money. Remember leveraged/margined trading is more difficult to get right than ordinary trading because you can make a lot of money or lose a lot of money very quickly, unless you keep your trade size very small.

I won't go through the different platforms individually because their lists of crypto products are changing so fast that any comment from me would quickly be out of date. So instead, go to my website (www.glengoodman.com) to see my latest reviews of spread betting platforms.

SUMMARY

If you simply wish to buy and hold a few different cryptocurrencies for the long term, you can buy them from a straightforward site like Coinbase and keep them in a safe offline cold wallet.

However, when I buy shares, I like to have a choice of hundreds, if not thousands, to make sure I find the most profitable opportunities. I wouldn't use a stockbroker who said "You can buy Apple, Tesco, HSBC or BP. Take your pick." Likewise, I want to choose from dozens, if not hundreds of cryptocurrencies. To take this route:

1. buy Bitcoin from a selling site/app

2. create a free hot wallet to store any surplus Bitcoins

3. transfer Bitcoins to a cryptocurrency exchange.

And that's it! You're ready to trade.

CHAPTER 5: MY MONEYMAKING STRATEGY

"There is the plain fool who does the wrong thing at all times everywhere, but there is the Wall Street fool, who thinks he must trade all the time."

— LEGENDARY TRADER JESSE LIVERMORE

DAY TRADING IS FOR LOSERS – LITERALLY

WHENEVER PEOPLE ASK me what I do for a living and I tell them I'm a trader, they reply "You're a day trader?" And I say "No, I'm not a bloody day trader!" And then they look a bit offended for some reason.

Day traders open and close trades on the same day, they usually execute many trades per day and they do not hold any positions open overnight. Day trading is a mug's game, and that's official. An extensive study was carried out in 2010 by a group of professors at

UCLA,* who found that of the hundreds of thousands of day traders in their sample, 95% were losing money. So perhaps by practising hard you can become part of the successful 5%? No, they also found that experienced losers just keep on losing. They concluded: for prospective day traders, "trading to learn" is no more rational or profitable than playing roulette to learn.

Since that study was completed, the balance has been tipped even more heavily against the day traders. We have seen the rise of high-frequency trading (HFT) conducted by computers that can buy and sell thousands of times per second. Trading firms pay millions for super-fast access to exchanges. This enables them to see the latest prices a fraction of a second earlier than Johnny Daytrader, giving them a crucial advantage in this hyper-competitive game.

Jesse Livermore, quoted above, did not become one of the richest men in the world by trading in and out of the market all day long. He watched, he waited patiently, and at the right moment, he acted. And once he had taken a position, if it was making him money, he would hold it, for weeks, months or even longer.

Day trading is a losing game because costs add up fast. Every time you enter a trade, you pay fees. On a typical exchange, you may pay 0.02% in fees for a market trade, so if your trade is worth $5,000, the fee will be $10. If you trade once a day, that's not a big deal. If you trade 50 times a day, that's $500. If you day trade 200 days per year, that's $100,000 in fees. And then the day traders wonder why they aren't making a profit!

And that's not the only disadvantage of day trading. There's also the spread. Day traders want to get in and out of trades quickly, so they place very large trades to make a profit from relatively small price movements. Let's say a day trader sees Bitcoin has a bid–ask spread of $5,999–$6,000. They think Bitcoin is going to rise so they buy 1,000 Bitcoins at the asking price of $6,000. They've

---

*   Barber, Lee, Odean, 2010. 'Do Day Traders Rationally Learn About Their Ability?'

already lost $1,000 on the trade the moment they open it (1,000 × $1 spread). Bitcoin then rises in price by $3 and they quickly sell their 1,000 Bitcoins at the bid price of $6,002. They've made a profit of $2,000 but lost $1,000 of potential profit because of the $1 spread. Assuming they're a typical day trader who wins some and loses some trades, those spread 'taxes' are going to seriously add up and eat into their profitability. Any competitive trading edge they may have will probably be outweighed by these costs.

Meanwhile, a longer-term trader (like me) thinks that Bitcoin may rise in the next few weeks, so I buy ten Bitcoins at $6,000 each, paying just $10 for the spread. Three weeks later, the price of Bitcoin is $6,200. I sell my Bitcoins and – like the day trader – I've made a profit of $2,000, but unlike the day trader I've only paid $10 for the spread, not $1,000. Over time, this makes a huge difference to the relative profitability of the two approaches. Quite simply, taking a longer view is more profitable (and generally a lot less stressful!).

THE TREND IS YOUR FRIEND, UNTIL IT BENDS

Remember this picture from chapter 1? It shows a typical market boom-and-bust cycle. The same human emotions drive repetitive market patterns year after year, century after century, in assets in every country in the world.

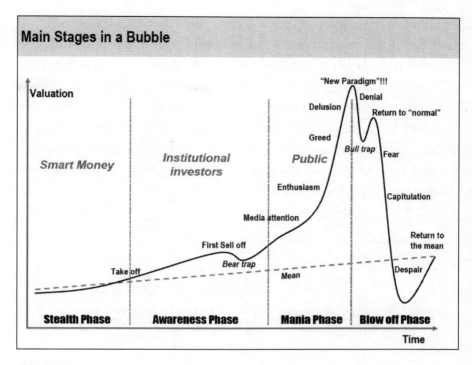

Figure 1

Source: Dr Jean-Paul Rodrigue, Dept of Economics and Geography, Hofstra University

For the canny trader, these cycles are not a problem but an opportunity. I aim to buy cryptocurrencies in the early part of an upward trend and sell them near the top. This means I usually miss out on a small chunk of profit at the very bottom of a price cycle because I want to see a new upward trend establish itself *before* I buy in. When I was young, one of my trading mentors told me "only monkeys pick bottoms". But inside that splendid faecal image, there is deep wisdom. Attempting to jump into trends before they've even begun is little more than guesswork. It ties your money up indefinitely in cryptos that are going nowhere. Far better to see the trend actually get underway and *then* jump on board. Don't try to be greedy by picking bottoms, you'll make more than enough profit if you jump onto a good trend in the early stages.

Far harder than working out when to buy is working out when to sell. You'll see relatively little discussion online about this topic – everybody's concentrating on what to buy instead – but when to sell is one of the biggest questions affecting your profitability. We'll spend more time on this issue in chapter 10. Just as I like to buy after a trend has already begun, I also like to sell after a trend has ended. Waiting until 'after the bend' is the only way to gauge whether the trend is truly over. The last thing you want to do is sell because you think the price has gone high enough only to find it then doubles… and doubles again! That happens more often than you might think.

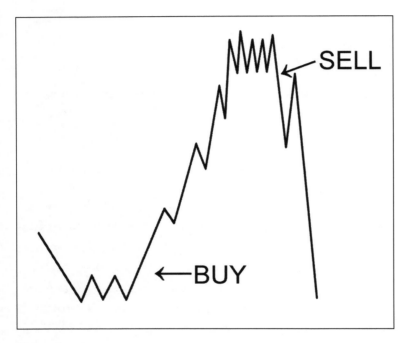

Figure 2

Figure 2 shows the typical entry and exit points of a **trend trader**. As you can see, they would miss the bit of profit at the bottom and the bit at the top but grab a hefty chunk of profit in between the buy and sell points.

Market price patterns tend to be *fractal* in nature, which means they repeat themselves at different scales.

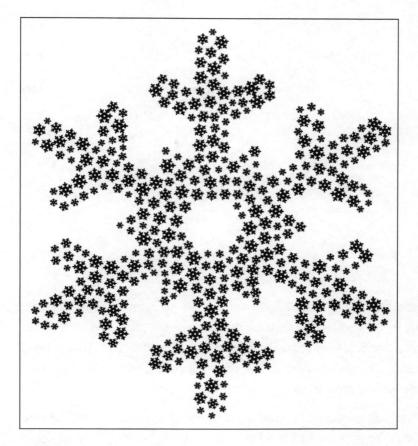

Figure 3

Just as the fractal pattern in figure 3 is repeated at smaller and larger sizes, so are patterns like the one in figure 2. A trend like that could just as easily be spotted on a chart showing a single day's prices as it could on a chart showing a whole year. The principles of trend trading are the same, no matter whether you're a day trader or a long-term 'position trader', but the costs are far higher for day traders, as I explained earlier.

Now let's look at a real-life example where I made a lot of real-life money. Ripple (XRP) spent much of 2017 bouncing around within a price range between $0.15 and $0.30. In mid-December it started climbing beyond that usual range which indicated a new upward trend may be underway, so I bought XRP, as shown in figure 4.

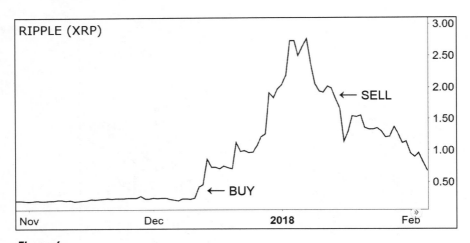

Figure 4

Chart by TradingView

In a perfect world, I would have sold at $2.50 after the initial trend reversal, but I wanted to wait to make sure the price wasn't about to go even higher. Once it fell below $2.00, I knew that the uptrend was almost certainly over, so I sold for a profit of 450%. Not bad for a one-month trade!

That chart illustrates the eternal traders' dilemma – how do you know whether you should hold on for even higher highs or whether you should give up and take the profit you've made before it all disappears? Every trader needs rules to help make that difficult decision, so we'll examine some of the best rules in chapter 10.

HOW DO WE KNOW FOLLOWING TRENDS IS A PROFITABLE STRATEGY?

How do we know that following trends leads to profits? Because there is a ton of research that proves it.[*,†,‡] We're lucky enough to have at our disposal more than a century of market price data from all over the world. Computer programs can easily perform backtests of different strategies to see how they would have performed over many past decades. I've tested a lot of strategies by designing my own algorithms for cryptos, stocks, commodities, government bonds and forex. Any basic, well-designed system based on following trends should make money.

The reason they work is very simple, but it goes to the heart of a huge decades-long debate among academics. The investment industry has long been dominated by the **efficient market hypothesis** which states that asset prices always fully reflect all the available information. In other words, whenever any news story breaks about a company, traders immediately buy or sell the stock until the new price is 'fair' once again, and this happens almost instantaneously. The implication is it's impossible to beat the market consistently because assets always trade at their fair value, so there's no such thing as a bargain.

Professor Eugene Fama of the University of Chicago popularised the efficient market hypothesis through his development of the

---

[*] Duke, Harding, Land, 2013. 'Historical Performance of Trend Following'. www.winton.com/research/historical-performance-of-trend-following

[†] Rohrbach, Suremann, Osterrieder, 2017. 'Momentum and trend following trading strategies for currencies and Bitcoin'. papers.ssrn.com/sol3/papers.cfm?abstract_id=2949379

[‡] Hurst, Ooi, Pedersen, 2017. 'A Century of Evidence on Trend-Following Investing'. papers.ssrn.com/sol3/papers.cfm?abstract_id=2993026

random walk theory which suggests that prices are not in any way predictable (they walk a random path), so trading trends profitably can't be possible. "If, as the empirical evidence seems to suggest, the random-walk theory is valid, then chartist theories are akin to astrology and of no real value to the investor."[*]

These ideas led to the tremendous growth of the passive investing industry, where people have been encouraged to stick their savings in tracker funds that simply follow the ups and downs of entire markets. The theory suggests picking your own stocks or other investments must be pointless because prices are already fairly valued.

Luckily for us, Professor Fama was wrong. Modern computing power has allowed us to test trend-trading techniques across decades of historical data and shown us that some of these ideas really do work. Trading trends can indeed be profitable, as even Fama himself had to admit: "Of all the potential embarrassments to market efficiency, momentum is the primary one."[†]

Markets are not efficient, because they are made up of human beings who have all sorts of irrational emotions that make them buy and sell, driving prices up and down – often very far from their 'fair' values. Markets appear to develop their own momentum because humans tend to herd together in one direction (FOMO!).

In 2013, Professor Fama shared the Nobel Prize in economics with his arch-rival Professor Robert Shiller of Yale University, who declared the efficient market hypothesis "one of the most remarkable errors in the history of economic thought".

Professor Shiller drew greatly on the insights of behavioural psychology, particularly the work of Daniel Kahneman and Amos Tversky, and the behavioural finance insights of Richard Thaler.

---

[*] Fama, 1965. 'Random Walks in Stock Market Prices'. www.chicagobooth.edu/~/media/34F68FFD9CC04EF1A76901F6C61C0A76.PDF

[†] Fama, French, 2012. 'Size, Value, and Momentum in International Stock Returns'. *Journal of Financial Economics*, vol. 105, p.457–472.

Thaler identified a series of psychological biases which cause people to make irrational decisions in the markets.

For example, traders tend to get emotionally attached to an investment. Let's say you research a crypto called Dodgycoin, you think Dodgycoin's a brilliant idea, you buy some Dodgycoins… and then its price goes down. The rational thing would be to admit you might have got it wrong. But let's face it, people don't often do that. Instead they scour the Internet for people who think like them and are writing articles called 'Ignore the falling price! Dodgycoin's just signed a revolutionary deal with Wonkycoin!' That way they can convince themselves their investment is still a good idea.

This is **confirmation bias** – the human tendency to decide on a course of action and *then* seek out more evidence to support our decision, rather than dispassionately assessing both sides of the argument. This causes people to make unwise investment decisions. If a lot of people all make an irrational decision to buy the same investment, it can push the price a long way from its fair value.

We are all susceptible to these biases and they matter because they cost investors a lot of money! We'll look at how to combat them in chapter 14.

What tends to happen is people get excited about a particular cryptocurrency and they buy it and that encourages other people to get excited so they buy it and the price goes up and up until most people start suspecting the meteoric rise is unsustainable, but they repress their fears because FOMO takes hold and they don't want to miss out on the cash bonanza. Eventually something pricks the bubble – it may be the most unimportant piece of bad news, but it serves as the first tiny snowflake that sets off an avalanche. Once the doubts start to be realised, the psychology reverses, hope turns into fear and prices gather momentum downwards.

We've seen all this play out in real time in the crypto market, with nearly all cryptocurrencies being gripped by confirmation bias towards the end of 2017, momentum gathering pace and prices rocketing. Around the end of the year, the bubble popped, the trend went into reverse and prices fell throughout 2018. At the time of writing, the selling continues unabated but eventually, when the selling is finally exhausted, a bottom will be reached and the cycle of boom and bust will likely begin again.

The simple result of these psychological biases is that **trends tend to persist**. If you buy into an upward trend at any random point, statistically it is more likely to continue upwards than reverse.

Trends tend to persist.

That – in four short words – is how I make my money.

WHAT IF THE TREND DOESN'T TREND?

What if a trend doesn't actually trend? This happens a lot! Trends *tend* to persist, which means they're more likely to continue than not, but that still means a lot of the time when you buy into a promising trend, the price will just go sideways or – even worse – into reverse gear the moment after you buy it.

This is where the **cut your losses** maxim comes into play. Jesse Livermore would ask "Is the price acting right?" Is it doing what you expected it to do? If it's not, you need to start thinking about getting out, even if you have to take a small loss.

The great thing about trading trends is that you only need a few really good trades each year to pay for a multitude of small losses.

DISCIPLINE, DISCIPLINE, DISCIPLINE

A great trend trader is like a professional poker player. They wait patiently for a decent hand to emerge, folding hand after hand with a small loss each time. All this losing can take its toll emotionally, but it is crucial to remain disciplined or you will miss the big wins.

During my trading career there have been times when I suffered many small losses in a row, making me feel so exasperated I threw in the towel. Inevitably, when I eventually return to my trading screen, I find I was just one trade away from a big win, and that I've missed the opportunity.

If you're confident you've developed a robust trading strategy, and you experience a string of losses, it might just be the equivalent of tossing a coin eight times and getting heads every time. It happens from time to time, and it may not mean there's anything wrong with your strategy at all, it might be simple bad luck. If you've examined your strategy and you believe this is the case, then it makes sense to steel yourself and keep pulling the trigger.

Many traders have learned these rules, but only a minority make money, because those behavioural biases start creeping in. A little voice inside your head starts telling you to break the rules. We all obey that voice sometimes, we're only human, but great traders learn to take the voice with a pinch of salt, to listen to it but ultimately to stick to the rules and **control the voices** rather than letting the voices control us.

TRADE THE TREND

GROW YOUR PROFITS

CUT YOUR LOSSES

CONTROL THE VOICES

CHAPTER 6: HOW TO CHOOSE A TARGET

"Those who have knowledge don't predict. Those who predict don't have knowledge."

— LAO-TZU, 6TH CENTURY BC

NOBODY KNOWS THE FUTURE

A s you explore the murky world of cryptocurrency forums, bulletin boards and social media, you'll come across a motley assortment of fortune tellers, soothsayers and general know-it-alls. These people have one trait in common: they know what is going to happen in the future... or at least they think they do. They will pronounce, with stunning certainty, that Bitcoin will hit $50,000 by the end of the year. Others will declare that Bitcoin will plummet to $2,000 by the end of the year.

They are all deluded, apart from this guy on my Facebook page, because he gets his predictions from the ultimate source.

Source: Facebook.com

The number-one sign of a trading charlatan is *big round numbers*. Now if they said "according to my analysis, there's a better than evens chance that Bitcoin will go up in the medium term" that would be fair comment, a *forecast* as opposed to a prediction, but if they say "Bitcoin will hit $100,000 by the end of next year" then you know you're dealing with a windbag.

And it's not just forums that accommodate these dodgy types. Wall Street is full of them too, giving newspapers and financial TV channels their predictions for where Apple's share price will be by the middle of next year or what the inflation figure will be in two years' time. Their predictions are worse than useless. Not only are they as accurate as a blind monkey throwing darts while riding a carousel, but they will cloud your trading instincts with their nonsense.

They seem so sure, you see, and we traders are only human. We naturally trust self-confident people, they seem like they know what they're talking about. You need to clear your mind of all the nonsense and focus on the task in hand – identifying cryptocurrencies that have a *good chance* of going upwards. There is no such phenomenon in the markets as a sure thing – if anybody tells you they have one for you, run as fast as you can in the opposite direction.

Luckily, all we need is a good chance of success, because – as explained earlier – if you hold onto your profitable trades and sell your dud trades, you'll end up with some nice big winners and some tiny losers. Even if you only succeeded with 50% of your trades, you'd still make a ton of cash because your profitable trades would be so much larger than your little losers. And you would like a ton of cash, yes? Then read on.

IDENTIFYING THE MAIN TREND

"In a bear market all stocks go down, and in a bull market they go up."

– JESSE LIVERMORE

The first step in deciding which cryptocurrencies to target is to identify the overall market climate. Many traders can't see the wood for the trees, they focus on the minutiae of choosing a trade entry point and fail to notice the general mood in the market is weighted heavily against any chance of success.

Markets have three main states:

1. trending upwards (bull market)

2. trending downwards (bear market)

3. trending sideways (in a trading range).

When the cryptocurrency market is trending upwards, it is much easier to make money buying cryptos. When it is trending downwards or sideways, making money on the long side is far more difficult but can still be possible. Some brave traders prefer to go short in down markets, a process we will look at in more detail in chapter 12.

The major trends I'm talking about tend to last for months or years. Figure 1 shows Bitcoin's main trends over most of its lifespan.* Bitcoin has always served as the bellwether for the entire crypto market, determining the general direction of travel or the "line of least resistance" as Jesse Livermore used to call it. Where Bitcoin goes, the rest of the market tends to follow.

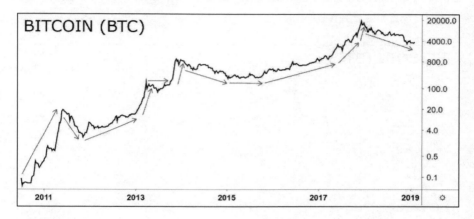

Figure 1

Chart by TradingView

If you're unsure of where the main trend is heading, many people find it useful to use **moving averages** on their charts. A moving average is a line added to a chart to help smooth out short-term price fluctuations and make the longer-term trend appear clearer. It is calculated by taking an average of the price over recent days. In figure 2, the thinner line is the 200-day moving average (MA) of the Bitcoin price.

It is a *moving* average because each day you plot the average of the past 200 days' prices (including the current day), so each day the

---

* I've charted Bitcoin using a logarithmic scale rather than a linear scale. As you can see, the prices on the right axis rise in leaps and bounds. This charting method lets us see how the price rises in percentage terms instead of absolute terms. It also allows us to see the trends develop over time, because on a linear scale the entire left half of the graph would just look like a long straight line ahead of a massive price rise.

new plotted point adds the price from the new day and drops the price from 200 days ago from the calculation.

If you average the price over only a few days, your moving average line will hug the price line closely, but if you choose a 200-day moving average, your line would reflect the average of the prices going back more than six months and so would often be quite far away from the current price.

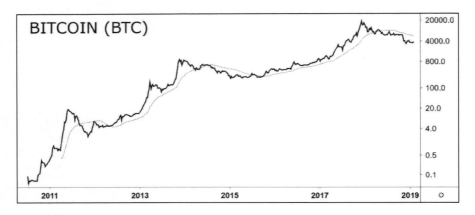

Figure 2

Chart by TradingView

By taking the average of the prices from the previous 200 days, the moving average line is always somewhat *behind* the actual price – there is a time lag – but it can help you to see the bigger picture. In the case of Bitcoin, the MA line is usually heading upwards, which helps you to see that – despite all the dramatic ups and downs – Bitcoin has spent most of its existence in a long-term bull market.

Taking a long-term view helps us to see the 2018 Bitcoin crash in its proper context, as simply the third major decline since 2011. On each occasion, the 200-day MA turned downwards. We will take a closer look at moving averages and how they can help you profit in chapter 10.

In a Bitcoin bull market, you will usually find the majority of cryptos heading upwards, so picking a few good ones to buy is like shooting fish in a barrel (but less messy).

Picking a good crypto in a bear or sideways market is much trickier but still possible. For example, in the midst of a market slump in the summer of 2018, I bought just one single crypto, Metaverse (ETP). Figure 3 shows the price plotted against the price of Bitcoin. As you can see, it follows Bitcoin downwards, just as nearly all cryptos did, but then it starts to buck the trend in July and that's when it grabbed my interest. I soon bought in and followed the trend upwards, even as Bitcoin continued to trend downwards. The price trebled in just a few weeks.

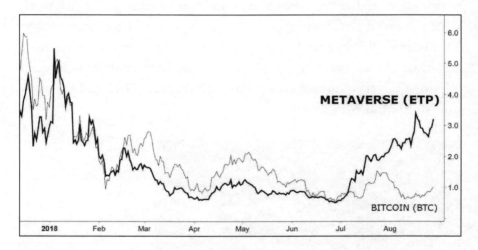

Figure 3
Chart by TradingView

PROMISING PATTERNS

There are two main schools of thought in trading – fundamental analysis and technical analysis. As mentioned earlier, fundamental analysts study the underlying factors affecting a price, the true 'worth' of an asset. This is very far from an exact science when analysing cryptos because it's so difficult to know which cryptos will become big players in the long term. It depends too much on which ones happen to become fashionable. Nonetheless, we'll do some serious fundamental analysis in chapter 8, as it may help you identify good long-term buys.

Technical analysis is the study of price patterns repeated across many markets and over time. This practice goes back at least four centuries, but the first definitive book on technical analysis was *Technical Analysis and Stock Market Profits* by Richard W. Schabacker, published in 1932. Before PCs came along, charting was a laborious process as each price point had to be drawn by hand, so Schabacker's book was an astonishing piece of work which showed dozens of patterns and explained what they meant. Thousands of technical analysis books have been written since then but most of the new analysis has been superfluous or misleading, so a lot of analysts choose to stick with Schabacker. They call his work **classical charting**.

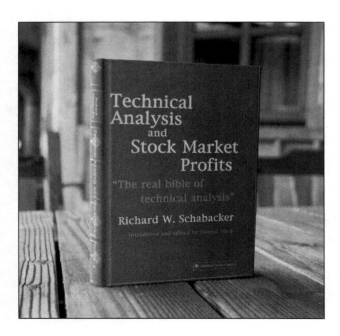

As for me, I use only what's been proven through empirical testing to actually work, and it turns out Schabacker's instincts were often right. Big data testing now proves that looking out for some of these patterns really can give you an edge in trading. They've certainly been a great help to me since I started trading cryptocurrencies. Cryptos may be brand new assets but good old human behaviour never changes, so those same old patterns are as reliable as ever.

CHAPTER 7: THE CLUES ARE IN THE CHARTS

THE FIRST STEP in selecting a target is to cast your eye down a list of cryptocurrencies that you can trade on the crypto exchanges you've opened accounts with. Click on each symbol in the **Ticker** or **Instrument** column on your trading screen and typically the chart of that crypto will appear in the chart window. You can then examine the current trend and any relevant chart patterns.

Many crypto exchanges use TradingView charts and if you go to the TradingView website (www.tradingview.com) you can use their basic charting tools for free.

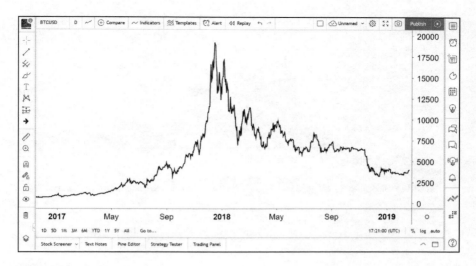

Figure 1

Chart by TradingView

The toolbar on the left of the screen allows you to draw lines on the chart and write annotations. The top menu on the far left is where you choose the financial instrument you want to chart (in this case it's 'BTCUSD' or Bitcoin priced in US dollars). Next to that is the time frame menu – it's set to 'D' for daily price points, but you can instead set it to show you prices ranging from weekly or monthly all the way down to the price by the minute. The **Indicators** tab allows you to choose from a variety of tools – including moving averages – that may help you interpret a chart and identify promising cryptos.

Now what you *don't* want to do is go overboard with these tools. You may have seen chart analysis online that looks something like this:

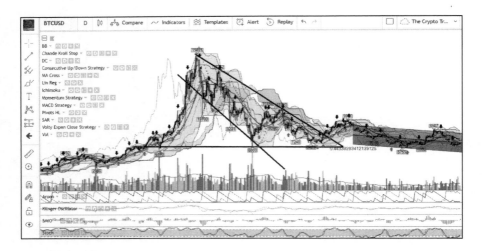

Figure 2

Chart by TradingView

This kind of complexity is a recipe for confusion and confusion is a recipe for bad trading. There is absolutely no advantage in complicating things too much. It's not big and it's not clever. Some of the most successful strategies are relatively straightforward.

CANDLESTICKS

And right after saying that, I'd like to introduce what may appear to be an unnecessary complication, but it'll be worth it I promise you. Instead of using a wiggly line to show chart price changes, we're going to use Japanese candlesticks, as shown in figure 3. They are believed to have been invented in the 18th century by a Japanese rice trader called Munehisa Homma who wrote the first book about the psychology of markets. The rest of the world only re-discovered his invention a few decades ago, but since then using candlesticks in charting has become standard practice. They tell you more about price movements than straight lines alone.

Figure 3

Chart by TradingView

A **daily** line chart is simply a series of dots showing the price at the end of each day, connected by a line running through all the dots. On a daily candlestick chart, each dot is replaced by a 'candlestick' which shows the price at the start of the trading day (the open), the highest price (the high) of the day, the lowest price (the low) of the day and the price at the end of the day (the close).

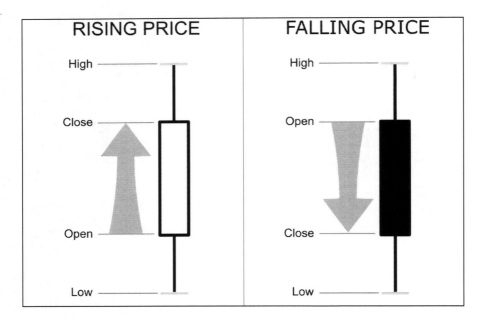

Figure 4

On the left in figure 4 you can see a typical rising-price candle. After the market opens for the day, the price moves around between the **high** and the **low**, and finally settles at the **close**. The candlestick is coloured either white or green to show the price rose during the trading day.

The falling price candle is given a black or red colour. The candle 'wick' usefully shows us the extent of the price movements during the day, outside of the open–close range. Later, we'll examine a particularly important application of the candle wicks.

THE PERFECT BUY

In late 2015, Bitcoin provided a perfect buying point. Figure 5 shows the setup.

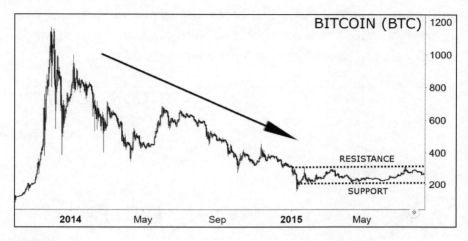

Figure 5

Chart by TradingView

As you can see, in late 2013, Bitcoin had an incredible price surge, from $130 to nearly $1,200 in less than two months! A boom on that scale is rarely sustainable, and sure enough, the price came crashing down soon after. Bitcoin was up and down like a yo-yo after that, but the overall trend was diagonally downwards for more than a year. Towards the end of the chart, the price starts moving in a sideways direction – it's forming a base, so we call this a **basing pattern**. The crash is running out of steam, selling pressure has begun to wane and people are buying and selling in similar proportions, which holds the price within the bounds of the dotted lines.

The top line is known as the **resistance** line and the lower line as the **support**. Whenever the price wanders down towards the support line, traders start buying in the expectation that the price will bounce off the support line, so the bounce becomes a self-fulfilling prophecy. Similarly, when the price approaches the resistance line, traders start selling in anticipation of a downward move, which pushes the price back down.

As a general rule, the longer this basing goes on, the more confident you can feel about the eventual breakout because the breaking of a strong resistance line is often followed by a dramatic move upwards. In this case the basing goes on for the best part of a year.

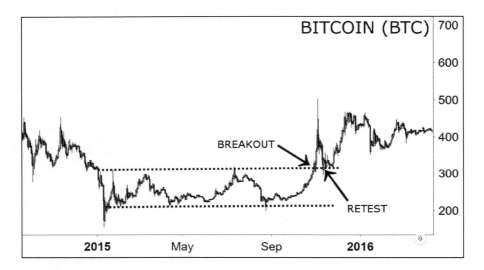

Figure 6

Chart by TradingView

The eventual breakout through the resistance line in late October was indeed a big move, but as is often the case, the price headed straight back down again to retest the resistance line. The retest can be deemed successful because the price hesitated at the resistance line and then resumed its new upward trend.

The rest is history and will soon be market legend. In centuries to come, traders living in Alpha Centauri will tell their eager trader children about the incredible Bitcoin market of 2017. There are few booms in history that compare with it.

Let's zoom out of that chart and see the big picture.

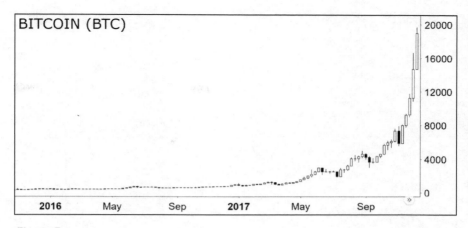

Figure 7

Chart by TradingView

Our breakout is on the far left of the chart in figure 7, can you see it? No? All that up and down action now looks like a flat line because it's absolutely dwarfed by the mammoth price move on the right of the chart. From that breakout point, the price of Bitcoin rose more than 6,000% in less than two years, one of the largest price rises in financial history.

DON'T CHASE THE BREAKOUT!

Now what if – for some reason – you miss that breakout point? Perhaps you don't spot the basing pattern until it's already broken out. Perhaps you're on holiday and only have half an eye on the markets. The temptation is to hop onto that trend anyway. After all, it's a new upward trend! There's plenty more profit potential, right? Here's how a regretful trader's thought process tends to work (figure 8).

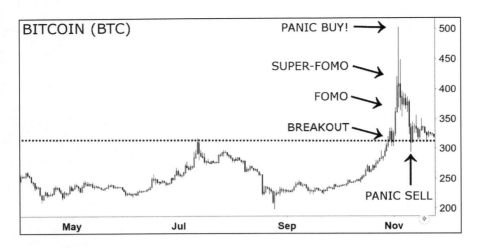

Figure 8

Chart by TradingView

They miss the breakout and the FOMO sets in, but they don't buy immediately because they reasonably expect the price to have a small correction after such a large sudden rise, and so they're hoping to buy during the price dip... but the price doesn't dip, it rises further. Now they've got super FOMO, but they're thinking it's definitely too late to buy now, they have to wait for the dip. But the price just keeps on rising faster and faster, and finally, after the price has doubled in less than a month, the FOMO becomes too much to bear. After all they might miss out on another swift doubling, and another, and another! So they panic buy, which inevitably marks the top of the short-term trend. As the price goes parabolic* the short-term traders who bought much earlier start to offload their Bitcoins to lock in their profit, and the price plummets. Our miserable panic-buying trader loses nearly half his investment in just a few days! He keeps holding on in the hope of a recovery, but as the price falls below the original breakout point, he is terrified he's bought into a massive price collapse and so he panic sells. As the panic sellers sell, the bargain hunters buy and the price swiftly recovers.

---

*　In maths, a parabolic curve is one which rises faster and faster.

And that, dear reader, is why chasing a breakout is not a great idea. You may perhaps be thinking to yourself that as long as you don't sell then it doesn't matter that you bought too late, because when the price finally recovers you'll make a fortune from the Bitcoin boom that follows. Yes, hindsight is a wonderful thing. The problem is by doing that you've broken rule number one: cut your losses. There's a good reason it's rule number 1 and not number 58 or 324. It's there to stop you going broke. Yes, in this example the breakout was a roaring success, but for every successful breakout, there's a **false breakout**, one where the price roars upwards as in figure 8, but when it falls back it just keeps on falling and falling, and then it falls some more and perhaps never recovers at all.

Staying solvent means protecting yourself from false breakouts. The best way to do that is to buy at the breakout point and set a **stop-loss** to make sure if the price falls much below the breakout point, you get out with no more than a small loss. A stop-loss is the placement of a **stop order** on a trading exchange, to protect yourself from the price moving too far against you. When you buy a cryptocurrency, you can then place a stop order to sell, which is only triggered if the price falls below the level you specify.

Now none of that means you have to buy the crypto the precise moment the price breaks out. A good rule of thumb many professional traders use is to only buy within 5% of the breakout point. If the price has risen further than that by the time I'm at my trading screen, then I usually disregard the breakout and wait for the next opportunity. Obsessing over one missed opportunity can make your outlook blinkered, which means you're more likely not to spot a new – and possibly even better – opportunity elsewhere.

RIGHT-ANGLED TRIANGLE

Chasing a breakout is clearly a big no-no, but that doesn't mean there were no further chances to profit from the Bitcoin boom during 2016–17.

The price didn't simply rise in a straight line for two years, it experienced numerous corrections on the way up, and during each correction a price pattern formed which provided clues to the next good entry point.

Let's go back to the breakout point in late 2015.

Figure 9

Chart by TradingView

The original breakout was followed by a period of consolidation where the price bounced up and down for six months. But it didn't just bounce randomly, it bounced in a tighter and tighter range, coiling like a spring in preparation for the breakout that followed. This tightening of the trading range formed the pattern of a **right-angled triangle**, as shown in figure 9. This is one of the most reliable setups for a breakout. But if it's so reliable, you may be wondering why I don't buy the crypto during the long period when the triangle is forming, in anticipation of the eventual breakout. The answer is, it can't be relied upon (*no* trading signal can be relied upon) and so buying during a sideways-trading period can lead to a lot of costly buying and selling. For example, if I'd bought Bitcoin at the beginning of April 2016, I would have been quickly **stopped out*** of my trade when the price fleetingly fell below the lower dotted line, as that may have been an indication that the triangle pattern had failed. Then I might have bought again shortly afterwards, only to be stopped out again by another of those downward candle wicks you can see on the chart. It is far better to wait patiently for the breakout to begin and then buy at the right moment.

If you missed the June breakout as well, all you had to do was wait until another one came along six months later, in December 2016, as shown on figure 9. Buying at $800 would still have allowed you to gain 2,400% profit before the bull market hit its peak! So when you tap into a decent trend, it's worth remembering that if you miss the first entry point, there may be more opportunities further down the line.

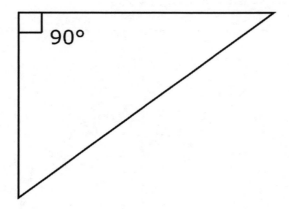

Figure 10

In trading, a right-angled triangle is simply a triangle pattern with a horizontal top or bottom edge. Statistically, these horizontal edges tend to be more reliable as trading signals than triangles

---

*   To be 'stopped out' means the price has hit the stop-loss level you set, so the trade has been closed automatically.

with diagonal support or resistance lines. Once again, this is probably due to human psychology. Traders' eyes are drawn to horizontal lines that appear to contain the price movement, while diagonal lines don't have such a definite solid quality about them. Horizontal lines feel like they have more meaning as support and resistance levels, therefore they do. It's a circular argument. The horizontal lines are meaningful because people expect them to be meaningful, and people expect them to be meaningful because they are meaningful.

SYMMETRICAL TRIANGLES

Triangles are very common in charting. Once you start looking out for them, you'll begin to see them everywhere. Unfortunately, as already noted, if they don't have horizontal edges they're not particularly reliable as trading signals.

Symmetrical triangles look like the one in figure 11.

Figure 11

Chart by TradingView

As they're symmetrical, they don't give much of a clue as to their future direction, but it's still worth watching for a breakout (in either direction) as the price approaches the apex of the triangle, because the eventual price movement can be quite strong, as is the case in figure 11.

WEDGES

Wedges are basically upward or downward-sloping triangles, also known as pennants. Figure 12 shows the Dash cryptocurrency forming a wedge in late 2017, just before a big surge upwards. Descending wedges tend to break out upwards, and ascending wedges tend to break out downwards. Usually they are **continuation patterns**, which means they are a short counter-trend reaction during the main trend. So you might get a strong trend upwards, followed by a short downward wedge like the one in figure 12, then the resumption of the main upward trend. A breakout from a wedge can provide a good opportunity to get into an already long-established trend.

But as I said, they are not particularly reliable patterns. You will often find that what you think is a wedge or sloping triangle morphs into a different pattern altogether. Also, they often break out in the 'wrong' direction. So while you're watching a wedge develop, just keep an open mind about what could happen next.

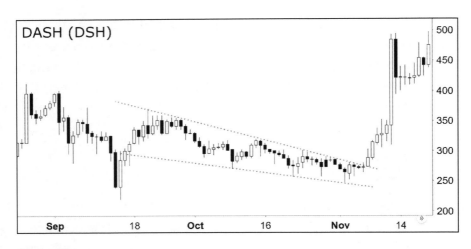

Figure 12

Chart by TradingView

FLAGS

'Pennant' was one of Richard Schabacker's terms. He also talked about **flags**, another common continuation pattern similar to the wedge/pennant, the main difference being it is formed of parallel lines. Figure 13 shows a continuation flag pattern. The price rises, then consolidates sideways – sometimes with an upward or downward slant – before resuming the upward trend. As with the wedge/pennant, the breakout point from a flag can provide a good opportunity to jump into an ongoing upward trend, particularly if the flag's lines are horizontal rather than diagonal. A recent paper from Hamburg University of Applied Sciences finds the flag to be one of the most reliable chart patterns.*

---

*   Karolina Michniuk, 2017. 'Pattern recognition applied to chart analysis'. riunet. upv.es/bitstream/handle/10251/78837/English%20Abstract%20Michniuk.pdf?

Figure 13

Chart by TradingView

HEAD-AND-SHOULDERS

The head-and-shoulders pattern resembles (guess what?) a human head and shoulders. Yes, I know that's silly and I'm starting to sound like one of those people who thinks the cloud outside their window looks like Elvis. But head-and-shoulders (H&S) is just a nice shorthand way of describing a relatively complex pattern. Empirically, it's one of the most reliable patterns with extensive academic evidence supporting its use to improve trading profitability.[*,†,‡]

Figure 14 shows what the pattern looks like in theory.

---

[*]   Osler, Chang, 1995. 'Head and Shoulders: Not Just a Flaky Pattern'. papers.ssrn.com/sol3/papers.cfm?abstract_id=993938

[†]   Savin, Weller, Zvingelis, 2006. 'The Predictive Power of Head-and-Shoulders Price Patterns in the U.S. Stock Market'. *Journal of Financial Econometrics*. www.researchgate.net/publication/31474225_The_Predictive_Power_of_Head-and-Shoulders_Price_Patterns_in_the_US_Stock_Market_Gene_Savin

[‡]   Lo, Mamaysky and Wang, 2000. 'Foundations of Technical Analysis: Computational Algorithms, Statistical Inference, and Empirical Implementation'. *The Journal of Finance*. www.nber.org/papers/w7613

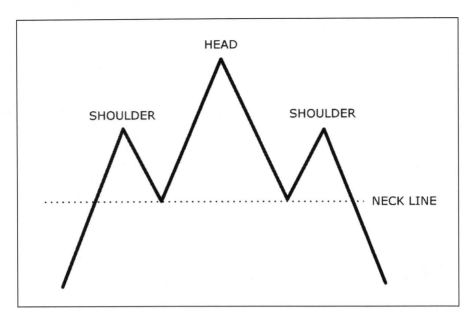

Figure 14

This is a **head-and-shoulders top**. It is a reversal pattern as the price is trending upwards until it gets to the 'head'. The formation of the second shoulder alerts you to the possibility that the upward trend may be over and a new downward trend may be about to begin. The **neckline** is where the price bounces back up after the first shoulder and again after the head. A breach of the neckline after the second shoulder marks the completion of the pattern and the likely start of a new downward trend.

Figure 15 shows a **head-and-shoulders bottom**.

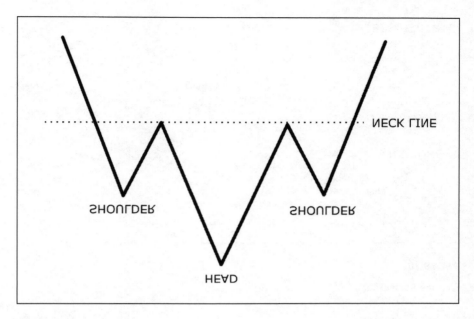

Figure 15

As you can see, it's a mirror image of the head-and-shoulders top, so I've simply turned figure 14 upside down (please stand on your head to read the annotations).

As with triangles, it's preferable for the support, resistance and – in this case – the neckline to be horizontal rather than diagonal.

In the real world, head-and-shoulders patterns often look far more complex and a lot messier than the textbook images. Figure 16 is Ethereum against the dollar during and after the 2017 boom.

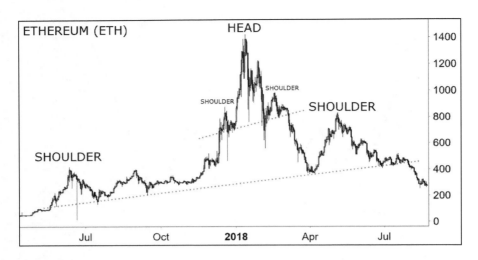

Figure 16

Chart by TradingView

What we have here is a small head-and-shoulders within a larger head-and-shoulders pattern (it's those fractals again!). When the neckline of the small H&S was breached in March 2018 that was a major signal of a change of trend and a signal to go short for anybody who likes to live dangerously.

As is often the case in downtrends, shorting was a real roller coaster ride. The price fell all the way to $400 before doubling again. At the second large shoulder, the price was retesting the neckline of the small head-and-shoulders. Then the new downtrend continued all the way down to the neckline of the large head-and-shoulders, where it paused as the last few buyers tried to drive the price back up but failed. When the neckline finally broke, support from buyers melted away, which allowed a more dramatic drop to take place.

Let's take a bullish example of a head-and-shoulders bottom (aka inverse head-and-shoulders). In Figure 17 we have a nice entry point for Bitcoin in September 2017, albeit a bit late in the trend. Once again, it's a complex small H&S within a larger H&S pattern.

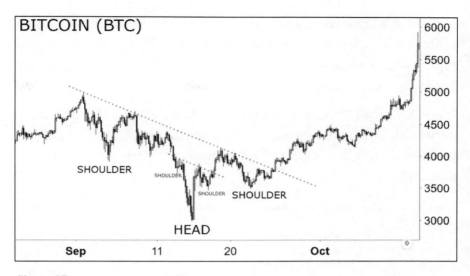

Figure 17

Chart by TradingView

When the small H&S was completed, there was a big bounce upwards to the neckline of the large H&S, followed by a retesting of the small H&S neckline. The test was 'successful' as the price rose again and broke through the main neckline and kept rising.

This head-and-shoulders gave me pause for thought at the time, because the slope of the neckline is pretty steep, which is not a great sign. But it held so consistently throughout September that when it eventually broke, I bought more Bitcoin.

CLOUD ELVIS

Many economists and others who have little direct experience of trading believe these patterns don't really exist and human minds are simply attuned to identifying patterns even if they're not really there (like 'cloud Elvis'). I can see why they would think that – on first appearances, technical analysis does sound a lot like astrology! The economists may scoff but they're simply wrong. The copious academic evidence of chart patterns improving trading performance is all the evidence we need. If rigorous academic studies proved that traders made bigger profits when the moon is in the 7th House and Jupiter aligns with Mars, then I'd be talking about astrology in this book. But they don't, so I'm not.

When you study historical charts, it's striking how often the same patterns are repeated throughout market history. Compare Bitcoin in figure 17 to the US company Woolworth from 1936, as shown in figure 18.

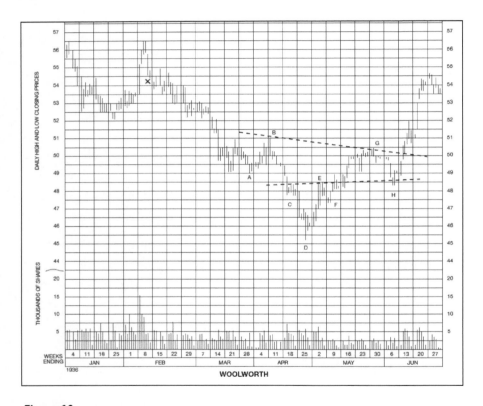

Figure 18

Source: *Technical Analysis and Stock Market Profits* by Richard W. Schabacker

The similarity is striking. Both exhibit a small inverse head-and-shoulders within a larger head and-shoulders. Remember, markets may change but human emotions remain the same, and that is why the patterns and the profit opportunities keep on coming.

DON'T JUMP THE GUN

Once again, you may be thinking you could make sooooo much more profit if instead of waiting for the inevitable break through the neckline, you simply entered the trade early. Problem is, there's nothing inevitable about the break. Sometimes, head-and-shoulders patterns fail, but when they do that can also be a good trading signal, only in the opposite direction to the one you expected! Figure 19 shows Bitcoin/dollar in early 2018.

Figure 19

Chart by TradingView

By early March, many traders had identified that head-and-shoulders and were itching to pull the trigger and buy. Some would have started thinking 'Well, what's the harm in entering early?' Those that bought before the break would have been sorely disappointed (and poorer), as the price rebounded off the neckline and headed downwards.

Once the price had moved lower than the second shoulder, it was obvious the head-and-shoulders pattern had 'failed', which strongly indicated that the downtrend established at the start of the year was likely to continue.

VOLUME

Apart from price itself, the most useful indicator is **volume**. If you're looking at a daily chart, volume is a series of bars along the bottom, showing the quantity of trading per day, as noted earlier. (If it's an hourly chart, then each price candle represents one hour and each volume bar likewise.)

Typically a volume bar is green or lighter coloured if the price has risen during that period, and it is red or darker coloured if the price has fallen.

In figure 20, the main thing to notice is volume tends to peak on days when there is a major price reversal, it tells you there is probably a major changing of the guard going on: if the bulls (the positive crowd) were dominant, then the bears (the negative people) are now in charge, and vice-versa.

We can identify several of these important points in figure 20. The 14 and 15 September 2017 (point A) saw enormous trading volumes and therefore a huge volume spike, as the negative trend abruptly changed to a positive one. On 12 November (B), we see the same thing happen again. 22 December (C) was another big turning point as the bulls and bears fought hard to dominate the market with huge trading volumes. On that day, the price collapsed from $16,000 to $10,700 and then went back up to $13,000. The market continued to recover for a couple of weeks after that. The last major turning point (D) was on 6 February 2018 as the long downtrend reversed itself and Bitcoin proceeded to climb for the next month.

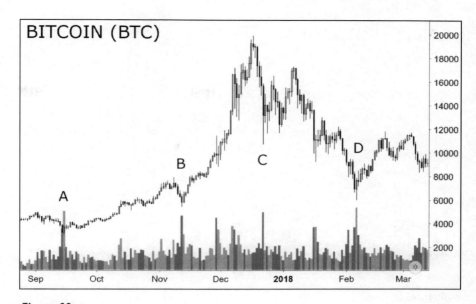

Figure 20

Chart by TradingView

Volume can also be useful in other situations. For example, when a chart has been quietly trending sideways for some time, a sudden breakout is usually accompanied by a large increase in trading volume. But if the volume *doesn't* increase, the breakout will often not follow through and will turn out to be a false breakout. An example of volume in action is shown in figure 21. Santiment's volume explodes in November when the price starts rising fast after a long slumber.

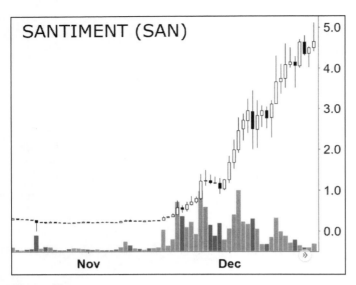

Figure 21

Chart by TradingView

PATTERNS INTO PATTERNS INTO PATTERNS

When we examine past patterns with the benefit of hindsight, it all seems pretty straightforward. You identify the pattern, you wait until the pattern completes, you enter the trade and then you sit back and wait for the money to come rolling in.

But when you're on the battlefront against other traders and you're watching a pattern in the process of forming, you may find your judgement is easily clouded by the opinions of other traders or simply by the uncertain structure of the pattern. You will often find you identify a pattern only to later realise it has morphed into a larger pattern of a different kind. It can be helpful to practise by examining past patterns as if they are still forming. For example, let's take Ethereum. In figure 22, we're looking at May and June 2017. You can see the price quadrupled in less than a month! After such a massive rise, we would expect a period of consolidation, and possibly even a full-blown crash, so let's look for clues as to what might happen.

Figure 22

Chart by TradingView

It looks like a symmetrical triangle is forming – so, as we know, that could resolve itself with an upwards or downwards breakout. Let's see what happens in July, in figure 23.

Figure 23

Chart by TradingView

So the price breaks out of the symmetrical triangle to the down side, but then quickly recovers and continues meandering downwards, forming what may be a flag pattern. This interpretation is not altogether convincing, though. Flags don't usually last so long, in comparison to the price rise that precedes them. I would normally have expected a flag like this to result in a big price breakout upwards before the end of June, yet here we are in July and the price has halved from the top point. I'm feeling wary here. Let's see what happens next.

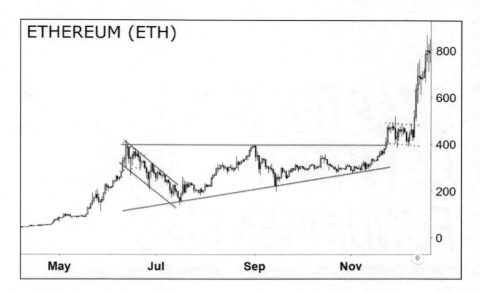

Figure 24

Chart by TradingView

Aha! And finally, in figure 24, it becomes clear. All these smaller patterns were all just part of the formation of a large right-angled triangle. By September, the large pattern was starting to reveal itself in preparation for November's breakout, followed by a small flag-shaped retest and then a vertical leap upwards.

So the lesson here is not to get too hung up on any individual pattern. Patterns represent possibilities, not definite signposts. Keep an open mind and accept change, transformation and pattern-morphing, allow the changes to alter your expectations. That way you will be ready and not resistant when the true pattern reveals itself.

CHAPTER 8: CRYPTO FUNDAMENTALS

"In the short run, the market is a voting machine, but in the long run it is a weighing machine."

— LEGENDARY INVESTOR BENJAMIN GRAHAM

A S YOU'VE PROBABLY already gathered, I'm not a big fan of relying on fundamentals for cryptocurrency trading. Without any revenues and profits, it is very difficult to pin down a crypto's true intrinsic value.

Companies that issue shares are easier to value. They produce quarterly or half-yearly financial results, balance sheets, annual reports. There is lots of solid info to sink your teeth into. Some investors specialise in finding little companies that have been overlooked because they're below the radar of the big banking analysts. Sometimes these companies are undiscovered gems whose shares are cheap simply because hardly anyone has noticed how cheap they are.

But for a cryptocurrency to become successful in the real world, people have to buy the coins or tokens in order to use them, and the very act of buying them will tend to push the price up. So a crypto's price will tend to rise along with its real-world success, which makes it very difficult to find a truly 'cheap' crypto. Traders will struggle to find such tasty mismatches between price and fundamentals as they do with shares.

None of this means that looking at fundamentals is a pointless exercise. You may discover a ground-breaking crypto technology that's not yet popular because it's at a very early stage of development, and if you're convinced it's going to take off, it could be a good long-term investment. But I would still caution you only to buy such a promising crypto if the price chart gives you positive signals as well. There are far too many examples of brilliant new technologies that end up on the scrapheap, and you really don't want your life savings to end up on the scrapheap with them.

Let's take just one example to ram the lesson home. Ladies and gentlemen, I give you... The Sinclair C5.

Source: Prioryman (Wikimedia Commons).

In January 1985, genius inventor Sir Clive Sinclair unveiled his revolutionary electric vehicle, designed to replace bicycles and small cars. It was cheap, zippy and perfect for shopping trips into town. It was launched in a huge blaze of publicity and captured the imaginations of millions of people around Britain.

Shame hardly any of those people actually bought one.

By the end of the same year, Sinclair Vehicles had gone out of business, leaving huge debts. Imagine if you had been a potential investor. You'd have examined the ground-breaking technology, the futuristic styling, the irresistible fun to be had with this unique new vehicle. You'd look at Sinclair himself, his incredible track record as the man who invented the world's first slimline pocket calculator and sold millions, then went on to invent the UK's first mass-selling home computers, the ZX81 and ZX Spectrum. By the time he dreamt up the C5 he'd already received a knighthood. Sir Clive appeared unstoppable.

But try telling that to the creditors who were left out of pocket after the demise of the C5.

Remember, there's no sure thing in business, in stocks and shares, or in cryptocurrencies. By all means, get breathless with excitement over a brilliant new crypto, but then calm down, catch your breath and examine the price chart.

Source: Alan Gold from Polbeth, Scotland (Wikimedia Commons)

CRYPTOFUNDAMENTALIST

Never describe yourself as a cryptofundamentalist, firstly because of the danger of trading purely on a fundamental basis, and secondly because of the danger of being reported to the authorities and sent to Guantanamo Bay.

How do we determine the fundamentals of a cryptocurrency? The first set of questions to ask are what need does it satisfy? Why would people start using it? How large is the potential market?

In the case of Bitcoin, you could say it attempts to satisfy the need for fast, cheap money transfers, it cuts out costly intermediary firms and allows people to bypass the banking system altogether, without sacrificing the safety or security of their funds. The potential market is everybody in the world!

The second question to ask is can it live up to its ambitions?

For Bitcoin, the answer is... possibly. There are difficult problems of cost and scale which still haven't been adequately solved (at the time of writing). Bitcoin works OK on a small scale, but once a lot of people start using it, the system slows down and becomes more expensive to use.

The third question is which other cryptos are trying to do the same thing? You will inevitably find similar projects, so do they present a serious threat to the success of the cryptocurrency you're investigating?

The fourth question is how many crypto coins/tokens are the developers planning to produce? The total supply and the rate at which new tokens are produced will both have implications for the price of the crypto. Flood the market with tokens and it will be difficult for each token to maintain its value.

The fifth question is how active are the developers on GitHub, the online platform where 'proper' developers upload their experimental code for other coders to comment upon and improve?

If the developers of a cryptocurrency aren't part of this thriving online community, you should probably start worrying.

And one more crucial question, well-put by Vitalik Buterin: "Projects really should make sure they have good answers for 'why use a blockchain?'"[*] A lot of projects would work just as well (or better!) without one, but because it's the trendy thing to do now they make their new app 'decentralised' by sticking it on the blockchain anyway.

To answer these tough questions, you will need to do some serious googling and try to really understand the specific technology you're investigating.

YETANOTHERICO

If you're more focused on technical chart-based trading than on fundamentals but would just like to make sure you're not putting your money into a scam, then most of your clues will be found on the cryptocurrency's own website.

We can illustrate this process by reviewing one of my favourite sites, yetanotherico.com. Take a look at the screengrab:

---

[*] twitter.com/vitalikbuterin/status/832299334586732548

Source: yetanotherico.com

You simply click on the 'Generate Another ICO' button and it randomly generates a fake cryptocurrency website for you. If you've spent time looking at real crypto websites, you'll know most of them look a lot like this. CurrencySquid.io looks pretty good, right? A "private public ledger" is exactly what robots have been waiting for. Let's click again...

Source: yetanotherico.com

Anything with P2P (peer to peer) in the description has to be a winner, surely? So what clues can we gather about DecentralizedDolphin. ai as a potential cryptocurrency investment? Well firstly, they've misspelt "5D printers" which is a bad sign. If nobody's even bothering to check the spellings on the home page, then how buggy is their software going to be? (An even worse sign is that there's no such thing as a 5D printer, but we'll let that one slide for now.)

The line of numbers is a countdown of the days, hours, minutes and seconds until their ICO, the day when they sell lots of their tokens to ordinary mugs/investors.

Scrolling down, we see their explanation of the product, with a pointed jibe about how dodgy cryptos often fill their websites with generic chat they've grabbed from Wikipedia or stolen from other crypto websites!

WHAT IS DECENTRALIZEDDOLPHIN.AI?

We'll create the first cognitive smart contracts for your 5D printers!

We'll change this market forever with emission of our useless tokens.

Token is a digital asset designed to work as a medium of exchange using cryptography to secure the transactions, to control the creation of additional units, and to verify the transfer of assets.

The last paragraph was copy-pasted form wikipedia and changed a little bit just to fill this block with some text.

Source: yetanotherico.com

Then come the professional team shots:

Source: yetanotherico.com

To spare their blushes, I've airbrushed out the smiley faces of the real people whose photos were used by the website. There is a serious lesson here: if you're interested in investing in a crypto, google the CEO and other main executives to check their credentials and their backgrounds. Who knows what dodgy businesses they've been involved with previously? Ideally you want to see lots of relevant technical and business experience in crypto or related areas. It's also a good idea to investigate the software developers and engineers, to make sure the cryptocurrency is being developed by people who are real experts in their field.

Scroll down further and you'll find the inevitable **road map** showing the development team's progress and their aims. Are their goals exciting but also realistic and achievable? Again, yetanotherico.com has highlighted a very real problem – far too many ICOs involve executives selling tokens with no real goals other than to enrich themselves and disappear off to the beach forever.

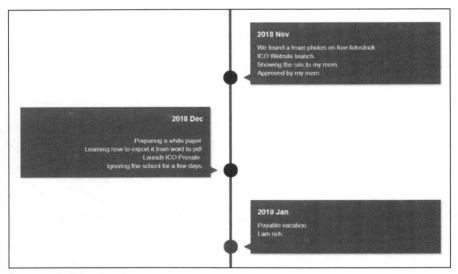

Source: yetanotherico.com

And finally we get to the real meat of the site – the documents. The **white paper** should contain everything a technical person needs in order to understand how the cryptocurrency will work. Sometimes a fake crypto will do a good job of blinding you with science. Even if you don't speak fluent geek, you can still open the PDF documents and look for tell-tale signs like bad spelling, bad grammar, sentences that don't quite make sense, failure to explain the actual point of the whole project. Once you've examined a bunch of these documents, you'll soon learn to tell the real from the fake and the genuinely intelligent from the pseudo-clever.

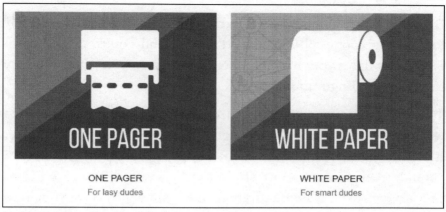

ONE PAGER
For lasy dudes

WHITE PAPER
For smart dudes

Source: yetanotherico.com

Frankly, even this joke website looks more professional than most of the real crypto sites I've visited. When you're sick to death of examining dodgy crypto sites, I heartily recommend a visit to yetanotherico.com to lift your spirits before you venture out once again to search for an undiscovered crypto gem.

ICOs

Investing in Initial Coin Offerings can be a quick route to riches or it can be a total disaster, but it is very hard to predict which way a particular ICO will go. Research carried out in late 2018 showed that 70% of tokens were valued at *less* than the amount raised during their ICO.* That represents a lot of ordinary people losing a lot of money.

---

* 'Burning Billions: Tokens Cents on the Dollar Against Raised Capital'. diar.co/volume-2-issue-38

That's why I generally prefer to wait until a new token is listed on a large public exchange and has established an upward price trend before I buy.

But let's say you come across a brand new project that you absolutely love, you've done all your due diligence and you're desperate to invest, but the crypto hasn't launched its tokens yet – then you may be tempted to sign up for the ICO.

The first step is to register through the crypto project's own website. Then you need to buy some Bitcoin or Ether and transfer it to your own private wallet (see chapter 4). During the ICO you should receive instructions about sending your BTC or ETH to the project's own wallet and about how you will receive your new crypto tokens. Hopefully they'll also provide some instructions about the best way to store your new tokens.

Be extremely careful that the ICO is genuine and not a scam website. Check the website address to make sure it's written exactly as it should be ('phishing' websites sometimes look identical to the genuine article but have one or two incorrect characters in the website address).

Bear in mind your investment money will have little if any legal protection once you hand it over. ICOs are usually entirely unregulated and there is no guarantee the tokens you bought will ever be worth anything.

Scary stuff, huh? You're basically handing over your money in exchange for a fistful of magic beans. But then again, that's exactly what they used to say about Bitcoin, and just look at that baby now.

NVT RATIO

The next few sections are quite technical (and a bit mathematical). I'll be describing some recent attempts to devise financial models based on the fundamentals of cryptocurrencies. If that sort of thing sends you to sleep, don't worry, you can skip forward to the **Social sentiment indicator** section.

Fundamental analysts of stocks and shares love to examine ratios that indicate how cheap or expensive a company is. These are not foolproof methods of selecting promising shares, but at the very least they may give you an idea of how far away the price is from a so-called fair value.

The most famous one is the **price–earnings ratio** (P/E).

$$\text{P/E Ratio} = \frac{\text{Share Price}}{\text{Earnings per share}}$$

This ratio calculates how many times larger the share price is than the profits (earnings) the company makes per share. Typically, a slow-growing (or shrinking) company will be valued at a P/E ratio of less than ten, while a really fast growing or over-hyped company may have such a high share price that its P/E ratio is up in the hundreds. A low P/E doesn't necessarily mean a company is cheap, but if you came across a fast-growing and profitable little company with a low P/E, you may just have found yourself a bargain.

Of course, cryptocurrencies are not companies with profits as such. Their value is in the growth of their network and how intensively it is used, so a crypto expert called Willy Woo came up with a ratio called **network value to transactions ratio** (NVT).

$$\text{NVT Ratio} = \frac{\text{Network Value}}{\text{Daily Transaction Volume}}$$

Network value is like the market capitalisation of a stock, i.e., the total value of all the existing tokens/coins of that crypto added together. Daily transaction volume is simply the dollar value of all the transactions that take place using that particular cryptocurrency.

Ideally, we would want this ratio to get bigger as the price of a crypto becomes more and more overvalued (because the network value is growing). But there is a major problem with this ratio. As previously noted, when a crypto becomes more expensive, transactions *also* tend to rise (because more people are buying it which means more transactions but also makes the price go up). So during a crypto boom, the NVT ratio doesn't necessarily rise as we might expect it to, because both network value *and* transaction volume are rising.

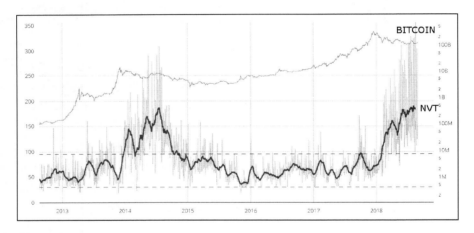

Figure 1

Source: Woobull.com

You can see in figure 1 that peaks in NVT tend to come some time *after* peaks in Bitcoin's price. This limits NVT's usefulness as a warning sign of overvaluation, but it is interesting that during a crash, transaction activity tends to fall away even faster than the price, which pushes the NVT ratio upwards. It was only several months into the crash of 2014 that NVT finally started to fall. That may serve as a useful indicator to help find the bottom after future crashes – when NVT has fallen back to normal levels, we could take that as a possible sign that the price is preparing to recover.

If you're curious to experiment with this ratio and apply it to different cryptos, you can visit coinmetrics.io where they have a working NVT model.

NVM RATIO

This is a more complex ratio recently invented by a group of Stanford University academics at Cryptolab Capital. NVM stands for **network value to Metcalfe**.

It starts with **Metcalfe's law**, which is a decades-old concept used to estimate the impact of a computer network. Metcalfe's law states that "the effect of a telecommunications network is proportional to the square of the number of connected users of the system". In other words, you take the number of network users and square it to find out how effective the network is.

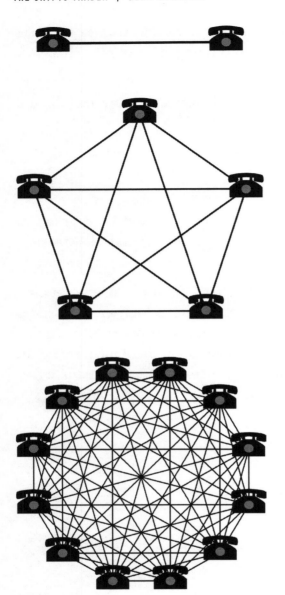

Figure 2

Figure 2 shows how a phone network grows massively in usefulness as each new user is added. If there are only two users, only one connection can be made, but if there are five users, ten different connections can be made.

Clearly cryptocurrency networks grow in usefulness in a similar way, and researchers noticed correlations between Bitcoin's price growth and Metcalfe's law as applied to Bitcoin's network adoption.* Cryptolab Capital combined Metcalfe's law with the network value concept to create the NVM ratio.

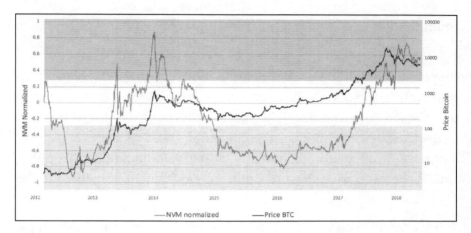

Figure 3

The NVM is similar to the NVT but tends to produce more of a forward-looking result. Whenever NVM enters the darker zone towards the top of the chart, that may be considered an indication that the crypto is overvalued. Figure 3 shows NVM flashed early warning signs of both the 2014 and 2018 crashes, as well as the major correction in 2013.

COST OF PRODUCTION MODEL

NVT and NVM are both demand-based models – they rise and fall depending partly on how many people are using a cryptocurrency.

---

* Ken Alabi, Stony Brook University, 2017. 'Digital Blockchain Networks Appear To Be Following Metcalfe's Law'. www.sciencedirect.com/science/article/pii/ S1567422317300480

Now we're going to look at a supply-based model. Economic researcher Adam Hayes wrote a paper about the cost of mining Bitcoin. He concluded, "As competition to produce Bitcoins induces more and more technological progress to increase efficiency and create competitive advantages, it might also serve to reduce the market price of Bitcoin."* In other words, as miners find ways to operate more cheaply, that puts less upward pressure on Bitcoin's price.

Hayes admits its not that simple, though. Satoshi Nakamoto ingeniously included a difficulty metric so that if lots of new miners are attracted to Bitcoin, it automatically becomes more difficult and expensive to mine, so the breakeven cost of mining goes up. Likewise, if the price of Bitcoin is falling, and miners are dropping out of the race, then Bitcoin's mining mechanism adjusts to make it easier and cheaper to mine.

Whenever Bitcoin's price is falling heavily, a cry goes out that a natural price bottom must be approaching because soon the price will be below the miners' costs of production, and if it's not profitable for the miners to mine then they will simply stop and the whole network will grind to a halt!

But the difficulty adjustment means that won't necessarily happen. If miners are dropping out, the difficulty falls which means mining becomes cheaper to do and so new miners join in and prevent the network seizing up.

Bottom line: cost of production ain't gonna determine Bitcoin's price.

---

*   Adam S. Hayes, The New School for Social Research, 2015. 'A Cost of Production Model for Bitcoin'. www.economicpolicyresearch.org/econ/2015/NSSR_WP_052015.pdf

SOCIAL SENTIMENT INDICATOR

This is not strictly speaking a fundamental indicator, but it doesn't need its own entire chapter, so I'm shoehorning it in here if that's alright with you.

Lots of companies are busy developing their own 'social sentiment indicator' for Bitcoin and other cryptos. These are all variations on the idea that a groundswell of excitement on social media will often precede a price rise.

One of the first to launch was the Bitcoin Social Sentiment Indicator from the Finatext team developing the Pipster trading app.

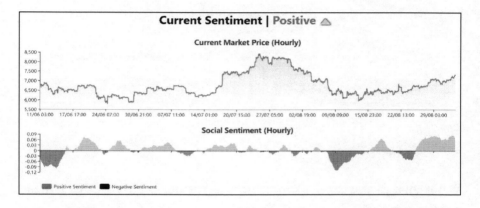

Figure 4

Source: Finatext

Developer Ryan Ong says:

> "The SSI tool effectively scrapes the global public sentiment of literally thousands of posts across social media feeds every hour. With applied machine-learning we can assess the public opinion of whether the community feels positive or negative, relating to Bitcoin. Given that cryptocurrency awareness and sometimes investment is predominantly driven by social interaction at the moment, this sentiment is a great way to see the trend of online thoughts."

The financial research company MarketPsych is another pioneer in this area. Its team developed a sentiment metric they call the MarketRisk Index, which quantifies the characteristics of speech on media and news sites, as well as social media.*

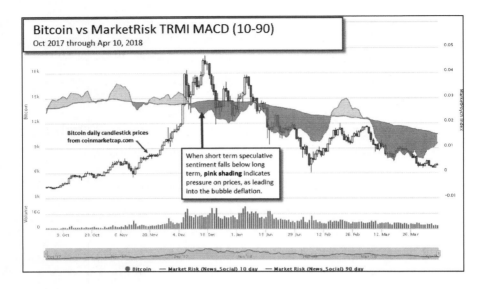

Figure 5

Source: MarketPsych

What strikes me after examining the results is that both of these sentiment tools do appear to have a degree of predictive power for cryptocurrency movements. Sentiment really does often start changing *before* the price changes direction. That is good news for traders like us who are getting into cryptocurrencies early in the game. These tools are very new, experimental and not yet widely used. Once they *do* become widely used, they may in fact lose some of their predictive power because the potential gains will be arbitraged away. In other words, professional traders will act the moment they see a signal from these indicators, which means ordinary traders will generally miss opportunities because the arbitragers will have snapped up the gains within milliseconds of seeing the sentiment

---

* www.marketpsych.com/newsletter-content/70

signals appear. But luckily for us, the pros haven't got their act together yet.

THIS IS THE NEWS

Some of the greatest professional traders enforce a financial news blackout in their offices. Yes, you heard me right – no news is good news, according to these guys. But aren't they trading in the dark? How can they trade without knowing what's going on?

The biggest problem with news is there's simply too much of it. Even top economists usually fail dismally in predicting where the economy is heading, because there are too many factors to consider, too many ways of interpreting current events. It is only with hindsight that economists can say "Oh! It was consumer debt that was the key factor, and it pushed the economy over the edge." But while events are happening in real time, it is extremely difficult – if not impossible – to work out whether it's consumer debt, unemployment, productivity or any one of a hundred different factors that will be the key driver of the economy in the future.

It's the same problem in the financial markets. Whenever Bitcoin is in a bear market, people look to the news for an explanation: "Ah, Bitcoin's falling because the Korean government may impose new regulations on the crypto market", "Ah, it's because the planned upgrade to the Bitcoin network has been delayed." But what's interesting is that when Bitcoin's in a strong bull market, bad news doesn't seem to matter.

For example, in September 2017, China banned ICOs and Bitcoin exchanges. This was *huge* news – China was the epicentre of global crypto market development, and now it was all going to be shut down. Yet, within a few weeks of the announcement, Bitcoin reached a new all-time-high! The terrible news simply didn't matter because the market was strongly bullish and nothing short of a nuclear war was going to change that.

Remember I was a TV business reporter for many years? Well, here's the reality of how the news business actually works:

> **News editor:** Glen, the market's down 30 points. Tell people why.
>
> **Glen:** But there's no obvious reason why.
>
> **News editor:** Then find a reason.
>
> *30 minutes later...*
>
> **Glen (on air):** The market's down 30 points today after the inflation figure rose again to what some analysts are calling a worryingly high level.
>
> *One month later...*
>
> **News editor:** Glen, the market's up 30 points. Tell people why.
>
> **Glen:** But there's no obvious reason why.
>
> **News editor:** Then find a reason.
>
> *30 minutes later...*
>
> **Glen (on air):** The market's up 30 points today after the inflation figure rose again to what some analysts are calling a healthy level.

News reporters have to say things – anything – that's their job, and they can always find some city analyst with an opinion that suits today's market movements. For reporters, announcing "Nothing significant happened in the financial world today" is generally a sackable offence.

So when you're doing your due diligence on a cryptocurrency you're interested in, by all means read the news and read a hundred different opinion columns but try to keep some mental and emotional distance from it all. Think of it as background knowledge and then look at the price chart.

The danger is that once you've bought that crypto and it's growing a healthy profit for you, you'll read some sensationalist news story or a nasty rumour on a forum and you'll panic-sell your crypto even though the chart still looks perfectly healthy. This is why many great traders try to avoid the news and the rumour mill as much as possible.

When a person loses their sight, it is often said their other senses grow more acute. Well, when a trader loses their access to the news, they may find they can read the charts more clearly. They can see the patterns and spot the true trends, without any misguided preconceptions or prejudices based on articles and opinions they may have read recently.

If something is going seriously wrong with the fundamentals of a cryptocurrency, you'll see it in the price, when the project's insiders start quietly selling their holdings and pushing the price down. Usually, the trend will start to bend long before the media report that something is wrong.

The bottom line is the price. Everything you need to know is in the price.

CHAPTER 9: MY BEST BUYS

Now you've got your analytical tools at the ready, let's run through how I made some of my best crypto purchases.*

SANTIMENT (SAN)

Santiment is a tiny crypto, under the radar of most traders, but it provided me with one of my largest profits of 2017, a 400% profit earned in less than a month.

---

*   In some cases I traded these cryptos against Bitcoin (e.g. SAN/BTC), rather than against the dollar, but the most accurate technical analysis is still done using the dollar cryptocurrency pair, as that's where most of the liquidity is, so we'll examine dollar pairs here.

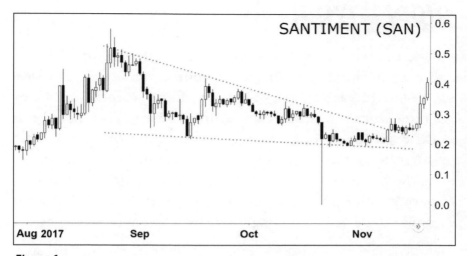

Figure 1

Chart by TradingView

An investigation of the fundamentals revealed it had what appeared to be bona fide management and a realistic plan to develop data analysis tools for crypto traders. Clearly Santiment would have strong competition in this market and they were not guaranteed to succeed. The token supply was capped, so there would be no future dilution putting downward pressure on the price. All in all, it looked OK, though I can't say I was blown away by the business plan.

What I was blown away by was that nice-looking three-month wedge you can see in figure 1. The price experienced a **flash crash** in October – a rapid bout of intense selling causing the price to crash – but it immediately recovered and settled back within the original wedge pattern. The fact that it returned to the same pattern indicated to me that the pattern was firmly established, and therefore was likely to eventually break out in a dramatic way.

I watched the price carefully but I didn't buy at the initial breakout point because it was very weak. The price hugged the breakout line for a few days before finally succumbing to buying pressure. The 'real' breakout then took place, I bought in, and the price doubled, doubled again and kept doubling until the beginning of January.

RIPPLE (XRP)

Around the same time, I was getting very interested in XRP, the native cryptocurrency of Ripple, one of the oldest and most well-established blockchain projects. It has huge potential thanks to the professionalism of the team at Ripple Labs. They have been working with major banks to develop new payments systems that may transform the financial world. There is still a question mark over whether XRP tokens will be widely used by the big banks who work with Ripple, and another worry is that Ripple Labs still controls (at the time of writing) more than half of those tokens.

Anyway, let's shove aside those long-term worries, shall we? Because, well, just look at that lovely wedge in figure 2!

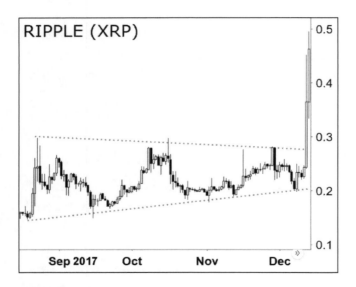

Figure 2

Chart by TradingView

Figure 2 shows the three-month build-up, followed by the price explosion leading me to a 450% profit in less than a month! As I sold all my XRP near the top, taking a handsome profit, worries about the long-term utility of the XRP token were not at the forefront of my mind. Once I'm out, I don't look back, I look for the next opportunity.

NEO

Far more than just a currency, NEO has been dubbed 'China's Ethereum', but it has some major differences. The founder, Da Hongfei, says he's building a hybrid system to merge the old ways with new technology. "We're not trying to replace the old system; we're trying to integrate with the old system. We're thinking we should build more hybrid solutions, not just those that are decentralized."*

NEO allows 'old' currencies like dollars, euros and pounds to be used in its system and it will have centralised identity certificates and legal compliance.

The aim of NEO is to dominate electronic contracts. Picture a future where most legal contracts are coded onto a blockchain. Critics argue that legal contracts are often far too complicated and nuanced to translate into computer code, but, to quote futurist Daniel Jeffries:

> "A contract is really just a bunch of conditionals. If this happens, then this happens. If so and so is with the company for three years, he or she gets this many shares. If someone violates this provision, this is the penalty. So it's really no surprise that legal frameworks are turning into actual code. Smart contracts are still somewhat primitive but they'll explode in complexity and utility in the coming years."†

By building a bridge to the old world of fiat currencies and legal compliance, NEO hopes to be the platform of choice for smart contracts.

---

* www.techinasia.com/talk/neo-approach-decentralization
† hackernoon.com/is-neo-the-one-67799886b78f

Because it uses national currencies, NEO's own coins don't power the blockchain's operations in the way that Ethereum powers the Ethereum network. Instead NEO coins behave more like shares in the enterprise. About half of them are still held by the company.

NEO could turn out to be one of the big long-term successes in the crypto world, but of course when I'm buying a crypto my feelings about the project's long-term prospects are secondary. My aim is to make money, not to buy, hold and pray.

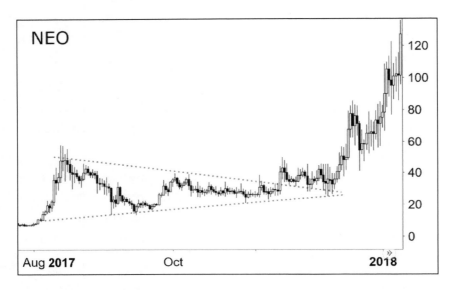

Figure 3

Chart by TradingView

Figure 3 shows a three-month symmetrical triangle. Because it's symmetrical, it doesn't give a clue to its future direction, but as cryptos were in a bull-market, an upside breakout seemed more likely. I missed the breakout (I can't remember why, I expect I was stuck in high-powered meetings. Or possibly playing *Angry Birds*.) As we saw earlier, chasing a missed breakout is not a great idea, so I waited, and luckily for me the price retreated, hugging the breakout line for almost another month before breaking out more convincingly. This time, I didn't miss the breakout. My combined

NEO buys across different exchanges gave me a total profit of more than 200% over one month.

If you're still tempted to buy and hold, NEO may seem to be a prime candidate for the long-term. So what would have happened if instead of banking my 200% profit, I had held on to NEO for the long term? Well, as figure 4 shows, by August 2018, it had fallen to less than half the price I originally paid! Instead of enjoying a 200% profit, I'd be nursing a 60% loss.

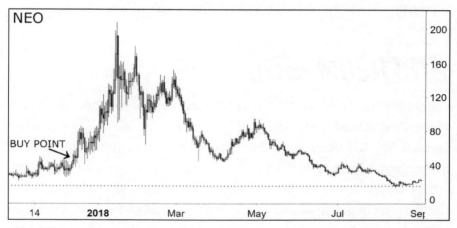

Figure 4

Chart by TradingView

Perhaps one day NEO will rise far higher even than its January 2018 peak, and if that's the case then I will make my 200% profit all over again! That, in a nutshell, is why I don't buy and hold, but instead ride the major trends.

BITCOIN (BTC)

I mentioned earlier in the book that we have this lovely thing in the UK called spread betting, and the reason it's a lovely thing is because you can trade all kinds of financial instruments with no tax on your profits at all!

Unfortunately, at the time of writing, most of the spread betting platforms only offer a few different cryptos to trade, which is why I spend most of my time on unregulated exchanges instead.

However, most of my trading in Bitcoin has been on spread betting platforms, I've made a lot of money out of it and don't have to pay a penny of tax.

We already examined some of the best entry points for Bitcoin back in chapter 7. A crypto in a strong long-term uptrend often provides numerous opportunities for a profitable entry along the way.

ETHEREUM (ETH)

Ethereum has been another nice little earner for me, and of course there is the added reassurance of it being one of the most promising cryptos for the long-term because of its fantastic revolutionary technology. Because it is so highly respected, a lot of new projects are being built using its platform and tokens. All of this bolsters the long-term survival prospects of the Ethereum ecosystem as so many independent projects now depend upon it. And in terms of Ethereum's management, well who wouldn't trust this face?

Source: Romanpoet

There have been many good buying points for Ethereum along the way, so let's examine some of them.

Figure 5 shows one of the first major price breakouts in Ethereum's history at the start of 2016. It's a symmetrical triangle so it could have gone either way but the upward breakout at $1 signalled the start of a massive bull market. There was a continuation symmetrical triangle after the first breakout, and this was quickly resolved to the upside in February.

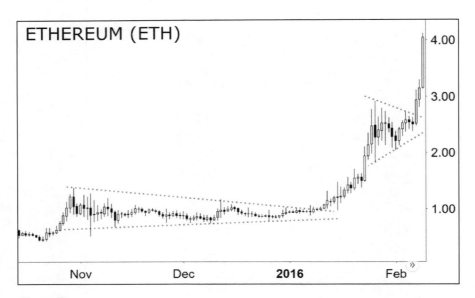

Figure 5

Chart by TradingView

If we zoom out to a longer view in figure 6, you can see the first two triangles are followed by a downward-sloping flag formation, which I've marked with dotted lines. This flag is resolved with another upward thrust, but the price then gets stuck at the February high point and the price meanders along, forming a right-angled triangle (which incorporates the resolved flag). At the beginning of March, the triangle's resistance line is broken with a strong breakout.

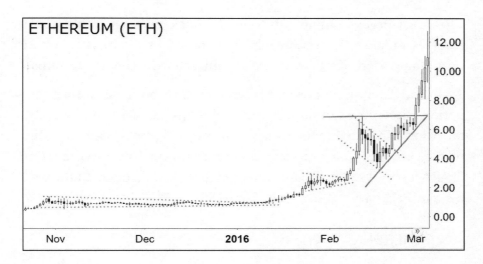

Figure 6

Chart by TradingView

The next phase, as shown in figure 7, is a peak at about $15.50. After a stunning rise of 1,450% in just a few short months, a period of price consolidation is in order. The price retreats back to the resistance line of the previous right-angled triangle, at about $7. It then recovers and forms a new, much larger right-angled triangle.

Figure 7

Chart by TradingView

The price breaks out in June, but – shock horror – this time it reverses quickly and powerfully. This failed breakout is followed by a long period of sideways movement which lasts many months.

Technical analysis is absolutely crucial here because during this period Bitcoin was in an uptrend and many traders were lured by the prior gains into buying Ethereum, only to discover it inexplicably refused to rise. Worse, it started falling until in December 2016 it finally reached the resistance line it had broken through all the way back in February (as shown in figure 8).

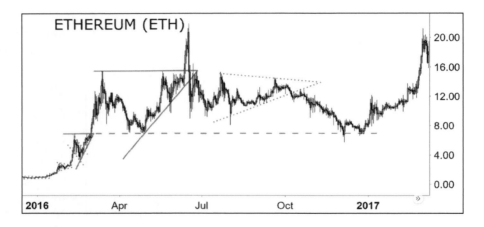

Figure 8

Chart by TradingView

Many eager traders bought Ethereum during the second half of 2016 at prices around $15 and had to endure a slow, painful collapse down to $7, losing more than half of their investment in the process.

But if you respected the technicals, instead of buying, you'd have sat back and waited, observing the symmetrical triangle until it broke downwards. There's no way you would have bought Ethereum under these circumstances. It's a comfortable position to be in when you're out of the market and patiently waiting for the right entry point. You can sleep at night, unlike the people who bought Ethereum at $15 and were still holding it at $7.

The first proper buy signal eventually emerged in February 2017.

Figure 9

Chart by TradingView

Figure 9 shows the price bounced off that prior resistance line, thus confirming the long-term uptrend was still intact, despite this months-long correction. The price then formed a right-angled triangle, broke out in February and began another dizzying rise. In figure 10, all the action of figure 9 is squeezed into a horizontal line (perhaps you can still just about make out the dotted lines of the right-angled triangle?). The price rose from the breakout price of $12 all the way up to $450 in just four months.

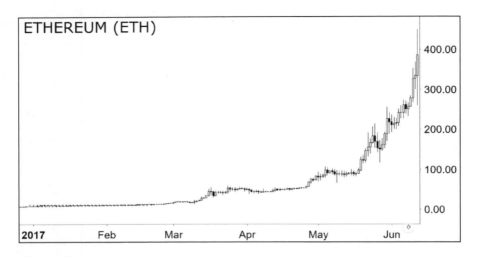

Figure 10

Chart by TradingView

After that precipitous rise, another long correction was needed – the market needed to take a breath as traders sold ETH to lock-in some of their profits. A six-month-long right-angled triangle (figure 11) led to one last big push up to almost $1,500 before the bull market finally ground to a halt. And so ended one of the greatest bull markets in the history of humanity. It's probably for the best as I'm running out of superlatives here.

Figure 11

Chart by TradingView

BUYING IS ONLY HALF THE STORY

After studying these examples, you'll have a good grasp of how to identify a promising buy point.

That was the easy bit.

But you'll get nowhere in trading without understanding when to sell. It's remarkable how little commentary there is on this crucial topic. Frankly, my buy-on-breakout analysis in this chapter is similar to that of any number of chart commentators you'll find online, but in the next chapter you will learn the arcane arts of deciding when to sell. If you google "when to sell cryptocurrencies" you'll spend all day reading a heap of terrible advice from people who know nothing about surviving and thriving in the markets over decades. Nearly all these 'gurus' were shouting "Don't sell!" in December and January 2018 – terrible advice which cost their followers most of their hard-earned savings.

The techniques you'll learn in the next chapter are the ones that allow professionals to make money year after year while (crucially) also surviving the big crashes with their capital mostly intact. It was worth you buying this book just for the next chapter alone (and if you're reading a pirate copy, then we know who you are, we've got your IP address and we're coming to get you).

CHAPTER 10: WHEN TO SELL

"The trend is your friend, until the bend at the end."

— THE UNKNOWN TRADER

S O YOU'VE GOT yourself a nice crypto. You bought at a perfect breakout point and the price has been rising for a few weeks. But then it starts faltering, the price whipsaws up and down for a while and then starts falling. Should you sell and take your profit? Or should you hold on for a possible price recovery? This is the eternal trading question.

And the answer is… there is no easy answer. There is no perfect solution to this dilemma. Whichever of those two options you choose, sometimes you will end up disappointed and frustrated. But the good news is there are rules you can apply which will make the decision easier for you, and while they can't take away all your frustration, they can stop you losing all your profits. Frustration you can cope with, extreme poverty is more tricky.

Figure 1 shows the chart from chapter 5 identifying typical buy and sell points for a trend trader.

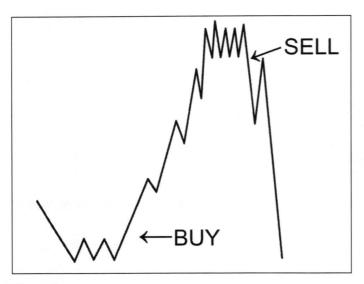

Figure 1

Some trend traders prefer to sell a bit earlier than this sell point and many would sell later, but the general principles are always the same – you wait for the trend to bend and then find a good point to sell. Let's look at strategies for identifying a change of trend.

MOVING AVERAGES

Many successful traders set up rules involving moving averages and sell when those rules are triggered.

As we discussed in chapter 6, a moving average (MA) is a line you draw on a chart that smooths out short-term price fluctuations and reveals the longer-term trend. For each day, it simply shows the average of the prices from a number of previous days, so it is a lagging indicator which is always somewhat behind the current price.

Let's suppose you bought Bitcoin on that perfect breakout day in late 2015. You can see in figure 2 that during the downtrend of 2014–15, the 200-day moving average line was consistently above the price line, which you would expect in a strong downtrend (because the MA is behind the trend.) At the beginning of July, the price crosses upwards through the MA line, which is a sign that the price trend may be changing.

Figure 2

Chart by TradingView

When the big breakout takes place in October, the price accelerates above and away from the 200-day MA line and that's an indication of a possible new upward trend.

The price then retests the resistance line. You can see in figure 2 the price actually spikes down below the resistance line, which some traders might take as a sign that they should sell, as they are no longer in profit on their breakout trade. Personally, I would keep a trade like that open because even though the price spiked a bit below the line, the price actually ends the same day back on the line. (The bottom of the candle sits on the line, with only the wick below it.) Where the price ends the day is much more important than any wild toing and froing during the trading day.

Obviously that would have been the right decision as the price then accelerates upwards again a few days later, verifying the breakout.

A trader who likes to follow long-term trends might use the 200-day moving average as a **trailing stop**, a stop-loss line that follows the price line at a distance, as shown in figure 3. They might have a rule that they will not sell as long as the price remains above the 200-day moving average. If the price dips down below the 200-day MA, then the trailing stop has been triggered and the trader would sell their BTC, either using an automatic stop-loss order they'd set earlier, or by selling the BTC manually.

This trader would not have sold the BTC they bought in October 2015 until February 2018, as shown in figure 3. Now you might disapprove of losing all of that profit at the top because the price falls from $20,000 all the way down to $8,000 before the trade is finally closed. But this trader bought at $330 and sold at $8,000, which is a profit of more than 2,300% in two and a half years, an incredibly successful trade by any standards.

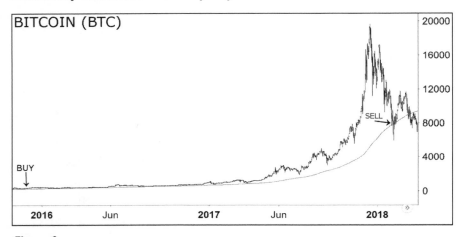

Figure 3

Chart by TradingView

Can we improve this result even further by changing the duration of the moving average? In figure 4 we use a 50-day moving average which hugs the price line more closely. The MA crosses through the price line earlier in 2018, which gets us out of the trade at about $15,000 instead of $8,000. But there is a new problem – the moving average crosses through the price line so many times, particularly in 2016 and the early part of 2017 that we would be opening and closing our trade dozens of times, which would get very costly, not to mention annoying.

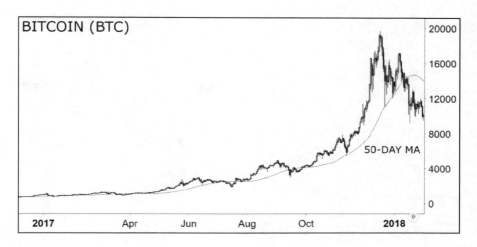

Figure 4

Chart by TradingView

Traders often get around this problem by using a **moving average crossover** system. Instead of buying or selling whenever the MA crosses the price line, they use two MA lines of different durations, and they buy/sell only when the two MA lines cross each other.

In figure 5, I've performed a backtest of an MA crossover strategy, to see how it would have performed in the past. I've used TradingView's programming capability to automatically buy or sell Bitcoin every time a 20-day MA line crosses a 50-day MA line.

The 50-day line is used to define the long-term trend, while the 20-day MA is more in tune with the ups and downs of the current price but it is smoother and less extreme in its movements than the real price. The advantage of this method is we get fewer buys and sells when we use two MA lines instead of one MA and the price line, because the 20-day MA filters out the more extreme price movements.

Each small up-arrow represents a buy and each down-arrow is a sell. As you can see, there are only a handful of buys and sells on figure 5 and the two MA lines cross quite early in 2018 which gets us out of the trade with a big profit.

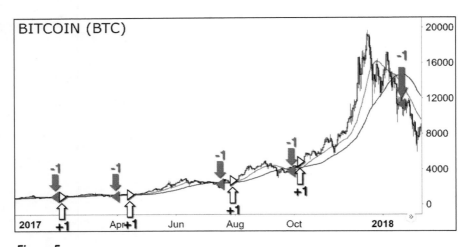

Figure 5

Chart by TradingView

Many traders like to experiment with MAs of different durations and perform backtests using historical data to find the holy grail of moving average combinations. The truth is there is no magic number of days for moving averages – you should choose MAs that suit the general speed of movement of a particular market. To be honest, such tinkering won't make a great deal of difference to your long-term profitability anyway. The important thing is to find a set of rules you feel comfortable with, because if you don't feel happy pulling the trigger, you will find yourself overruling your system, however wonderful it is in theory.

AVERAGE TRUE RANGE

Another viable trailing stop is based on **average true range** (ATR). This is a really useful concept and we'll return to it later on when we discuss how much money to put into each crypto trade. But for now, we're just going to use it to help us design a trailing stop.

Average true range measures price volatility. In other words, it's a gauge of how wildly (or calmly) the price tends to move up and down each day. It's a bit of a complex calculation, but roughly speaking, if you use an ATR of 20 on your chart, that means it's measuring the price-movement-per-day, averaged over the past 20 days.

I've plotted a typical ATR trailing stop in figure 6. Here I'm using a 30-day ATR, and in order to keep the ATR trailing stop line comfortably far away from the price line, traders often subtract a *multiple* of the ATR from the highest price reached in recent days, so in figure 6 I'm subtracting five times the ATR.

ATR trailing stop = Highest price in the last 30 days − (5 × ATR)

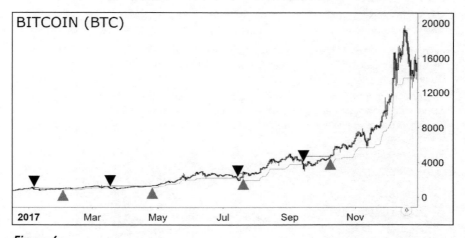

Figure 6

Chart by TradingView

This kind of stop is sometimes called a **chandelier stop** – and, as you can see, it didn't involve much buying and selling during 2017, and it got us out of the trade at about $14,000. Not a bad result.

THE SENTIENT ANDROID

I used to use MA and ATR trailing stops like those in the sections above, but as I developed as a trader I found I no longer needed to rely on these blunt mathematical tools. I started to develop a natural feel for the ebb and flow of the markets, so I started choosing my own exit points, which were generally pretty similar to the MA and ATR exit points anyway. MA and ATR stops are often used in algorithms designed for automatic system trading so I guess you could say I started thinking like a sentient android, trading like a robot with a dash of human intuition thrown into the mix.

Figure 7 is probably the best example of my approach. (Yes, I know I showed you this Facebook post earlier in the book, but as it was one of the best market timing shouts of my career, I'm going to milk it for all it's worth.)

The Shares Guy
Published by Glen Goodman [?] · December 24, 2017 · 🌐

In some of my videos, I talked about how Bitcoin's price was rising like a classic "exponential curve". This week the price broke down through that curve.

This is a warning sign. The risks of investing are now greater. The price may perhaps rise again, perhaps even higher than ever before, but that nice, smooth, predictable two-year-price-rise is over now and nobody can know where the price will go next.

Figure 7

Source: www.facebook.com/thesharesguy

Because the Bitcoin market has risen so steeply over time, it's much easier to view the long-term trends using a logarithmic chart, as mentioned earlier. Log charts allow us to see *percentage changes* in price rather than *absolute prices*. For example, in figure 8, the vertical distance between $20 and $60 is the same as the distance between $200 and $600 and is the same as the distance between $2,000 and $6,000.

A lot of technical traders rely on drawing trend lines to identify trends, which would be fine if markets rose in nice straight lines. Unfortunately, most of the time they don't.

The first dotted line on the left-hand side of figure 8 is the trend line many early Bitcoin enthusiasts were excitedly drawing on their log charts back in 2011, saying it represented the direction of the 'true' long-term trend. The idea is when the price deviates far from the trend line, it will eventually return to the path of the true trend. As you can see, it didn't remain valid for long. The trend line was definitively broken in late 2011 and the price never returned to that dotted path again.

Many traders made the same mistake in 2012–14, believing the second dotted line was the real trend of Bitcoin. But it wasn't.

They were at it yet again in 2017–18, declaring the third dotted line was the line we would follow "to the moon!"

The lesson here is: use trend lines with caution. Don't get too attached to nice straight trend lines, they are sometimes more misleading than they are illuminating. The main problem is it's too easy to place a trend line wherever it suits you to put it, so it can simply reinforce a prejudice you may have in favour of a particular trend direction.

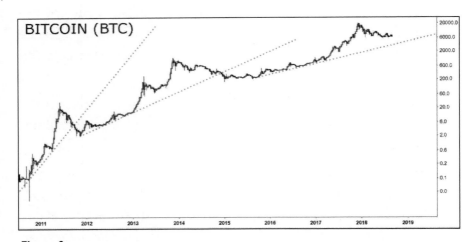

Figure 8

Chart by TradingView

The real long-term trend of Bitcoin is visible to anyone who simply stands back and looks objectively at the price line in figure 8. It doesn't require any trendlines or moving averages to describe. It's so simple I can draw it freehand on Microsoft Paint. It looks vaguely like a set of cow's udders. See, I've even drawn on the teats for you.

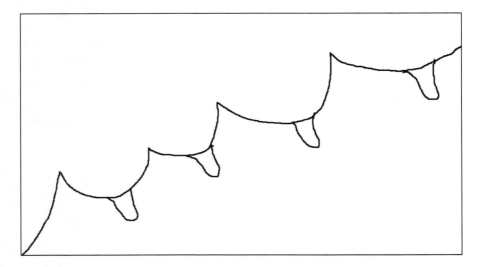

Figure 9

What we're really looking at is just a series of waves. Spend some time on the seashore, watching the ebb and flow of the tide, and you'll soon feel the similarity to the markets. Of course, the reason for the similarity is the ebb and flow of human emotions causes the market waves to take these shapes. Riding these waves expertly is the route to big profits.

Throughout their existence, Bitcoin and cryptocurrency prices have been characterised by a series of dramatic tidal waves that rise to a vertical peak and then crash mercilessly. These can to some extent be modelled and even predicted mathematically by an equation called the **log-periodic power law.**[*]

But just because that's how cryptocurrencies have behaved so far, that doesn't mean the pattern of exponential growth followed by sudden crash will continue indefinitely. Many price booms in other markets resemble other types of curve, such as the classic **bell curve** (figure 10).

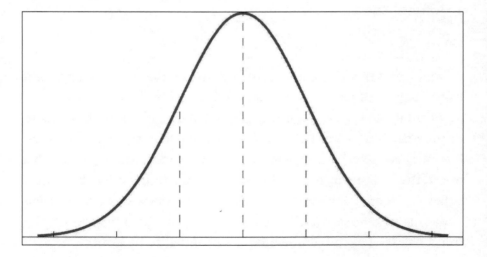

Figure 10

---

[*]   Emile Jacobsson, Stockholm University, 2009. 'How to predict crashes in financial markets with the Log-Periodic Power Law'. www2.math.su.se/matstat/reports/serieb/2009/rep7/report.pdf

The dotcom boom and bust at the start of the millennium was a more gentle kind of crash (though it certainly didn't feel like it at the time!). The market provided ample warning of disaster for anybody who knew what they were doing (sadly, at the time, I wasn't one of those people). The performance of the S&P 500 index of leading US shares is shown in figure 11.

Figure 11

Chart by TradingView

As I look at it now, it's clear to me that the market is not acting right from the point I have marked 'danger!' It has broken down through its normal trading range, but it is not quite scary enough for us to declare the long-term uptrend over. Only when we reach the point I've marked 'sell' do things start to look seriously not right. By this point, the long-term uptrend looks very much like it has become a sideways trend, or possibly even the start of a new downward trend (which is of course what it turned out to be). In other words, the trend has started to bend, which is our signal to bail out.

Let's now draw some lines on the chart and see if technical analysis backs up what my eyes are telling me.

Figure 12

Chart by TradingView

The two dotted lines form an ascending wedge which broke downwards at the point I identified as 'danger'. The price then goes on to form a classic head-and-shoulders top, with the neckline marked by the dashes. The point I identified as the 'sell' point where the trend is bending also happens to be where the head and shoulders breaks downwards. The price then rebounds upwards to retest the neckline before collapsing further.

In other words, the dotcom collapse was perfectly predictable for a trend trader! If only I'd been one at the time.

Luckily, I was a trend trader by the time the 2008 collapse came along, and I took full advantage, as I recounted in chapter 3. Let's take a moment to examine the S&P 500 chart from 2008.

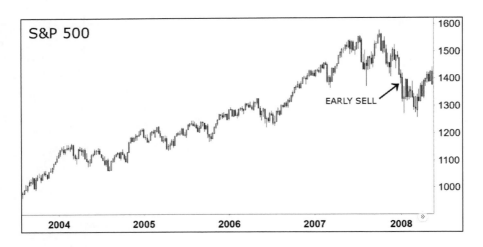

Figure 13

Chart by TradingView

As the market began to bend in 2007, I gradually sold my shares. I did this gradually because I respected the individual chart of each share, as well as the chart for the overall market. I waited until each company's own share chart indicated a serious bend in the trend before I sold that share.

My view of the market at that time was biased by my belief that the subprime loan problems in the US would cause a catastrophic banking collapse. That's why I jumped the gun by shorting banking shares at the point I've marked as 'early sell' on figure 13.

Initially I turned my £3,000 stake into £15,000 but after the initial market fall, as you can see, the market rose even higher than my initial sell point and I almost lost the lot.

My mistake was to go short while the market was still – just about – in an uptrend. The dam had not yet broken and I almost ended up flat broke by pulling the trigger a little bit too early.

But then this happened (figure 14) and my £3,000 stake turned into £100,000, so I lived to tell my story to the newspapers. I wonder how many other people made the same mistake as me but didn't quite manage to stay solvent long enough? You never hear about those people because they're too busy stacking shelves in Tesco. I took a wild risk and was damned lucky it paid off.

Whenever you read a story about a trader who turned his student loan into £1m (invariably it's a he), just remember that was a hugely lucky gamble and you're only reading about the one student who was lucky, not the thousand other students who lost their entire student loans in the markets.

Figure 14

Chart by TradingView

During an upward trend, I have in the back of my mind all the geometric shapes that typify the normal price movement I would expect in a strong trend. If the trend deviates significantly from my expectations, I will start to twitch my finger towards that sell button. As Jesse Livermore used to say *"As long as a stock is acting right, and the market is right, do not be in a hurry to take profits."*

---

*   *How To Trade In Stocks*, Jesse Livermore, 1940.

RIDING THE WAVES

Let's look at how exactly to remain in a trend until it bends. As a case study, we'll use that incredible 2015–17 Bitcoin boom again (yes I can't get enough of it). Instead of using MAs or ATR trailing stops, I simply try to respect the natural rhythms or waves of the market. Support and resistance lines are very useful for this purpose.

In figure 15 the lowest dotted line is the initial breakout line you may remember from our earlier analysis, the breakout that marks the beginning of the two-year uptrend. An ascending triangle then forms and when the next breakout occurs (in June 2016) the top line of the triangle which acted as the resistance line now becomes the new support line.

Then another ascending triangle forms, it breaks out in November and again the resistance becomes the new support (at just below $800). The price falls sharply from nearly $1,200 back to the support line, but only the wick of the candle spikes downwards below the support, and the price ends the day back on the line, indicating that the support has just about managed to hold.

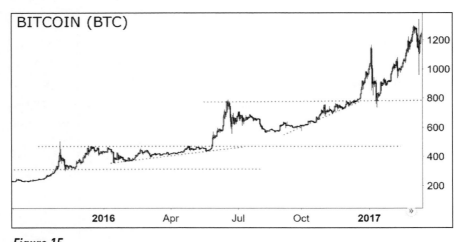

Figure 15

Chart by TradingView

Had the price continued downwards below $800 the following day, I would have sold my BTC and taken my profit, as the definitive break of the support line would have been a strong warning. Novice traders often protest at this suggestion, saying "What a waste! You should just wait for the price to go back up!" But it is imperative to recognise that a badly broken support line may be just the beginning. Sometimes a price will then continue to plummet all the way down until your profit has vaporised! A savvy trader has to know when to cash in his/her chips as all trends have to end sometime.

In the case of Bitcoin, though – as we've observed – the support line was not definitively broken, so let's continue our analysis in figure 16.

Figure 16

Chart by TradingView

Now this is where we encounter our first really tricky decision. The market continues to remain comfortably above the $800 support line and then accelerates upwards, tripling in value between March and June. After such an astonishing rise, we would expect a period of consolidation – and indeed, in June the price forms a symmetrical triangle, but in July the price breaks out *downwards*, which is worrying. It falls sharply, dipping below $2,000, which means it has lost more than a third of its value from its $3,000 peak.

Many trend traders (including me) would be tempted to sell at about $2,400, as the price breaks downwards out of that triangle. It would make no sense to hold on to BTC as the price falls all the way back to the previous support level at $800!

But luckily, there is another sort-of-support line before that. It's marked by the dashed line at $1,800 and is defined by the low point of the brief decline in May, when the price spikes down to $1,800.

In July, the price again spikes down and tests that $1,800 support line – which no doubt gives millions of Bitcoin investors a sleepless night – but the line holds firm and the price bounces back up, forming a nice horizontal flag before continuing its upward trend in August.

The top line of the flag becomes the new support. It is briefly tested in September before the price continues its rise, gathering even more momentum.

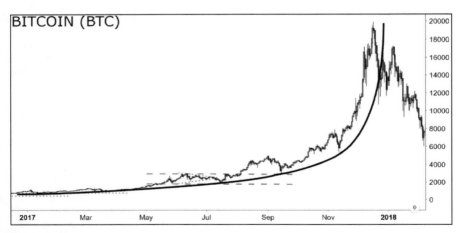

Figure 17

Chart by TradingView

The bull trend has now lasted 18 months and is rising faster and faster, so it's possible to draw a curve to infinity tracking that explosive growth.

Of course, in the real world, prices don't accelerate to infinity, they crash instead, and so the point at which the price breaks that curve is a major warning sign, as I pointed out in my Christmas Eve Facebook post. As per Jesse Livermore, the price was no longer acting right.

At that point I was starting to sell some of my crypto holdings, but only cautiously as it was possible the trend could still recover from this setback.

In January the price made a failed attempt to reach $20,000 again and then fell even further than before. This was all the confirmation I needed. It was highly unlikely the bull market could resume now, so I was soon selling all my crypto assets. I didn't sell my other cryptos purely because Bitcoin's bull market was over – instead I waited for each individual crypto to show its own signs of reversing downwards before I sold, just in case any of them managed to buck the downward pressure.

WHEN TO CUT YOUR LOSSES

Exiting a successful trade can be a painful decision, but the real pain comes from cutting your losses on *failed* trades, because you will have to do it over and over (and over) again for as long as you're a trader.

The aim is to make it as swift, simple and automatic as ripping off a plaster. Whenever you enter a trade, you should decide where you would exit the trade if it fails to act right. As a rough rule of thumb, many successful traders choose not to risk more than 0.5 to 1% of their trading capital on a single trade. This may seem pathetically low if you're a big-betting novice trader, but keep betting big and some day soon you won't be able to bet at all.

Ideally you should choose a stop-loss point that makes sense from a charting point of view. For example, in figure 18, Dash is setting up nicely in early 2015, with an ascending triangle forming.

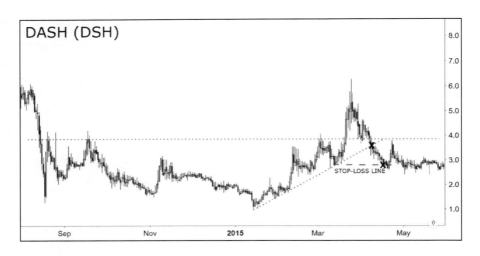

Figure 18

Chart by TradingView

The price breaks out in March and a natural place to put a stop-loss would be along the lower triangle edge. Alternatively, a wider stop could be placed at $3.00 because that's the most recent low point (where the price touched the bottom of the sloping triangle edge in early March, just before the breakout). You may wish simply to keep a close eye on the price or you can place a stop-loss order. (Remember, on most crypto platforms you will be able to place an order which will be automatically triggered when the price falls below the specified level.)

After the price breaks out in March 2015, it fails to breach the previous resistance level (at $6 in August 2014) and retreats back down. It retests the breakout line and looks as if it might take off upwards again but then it falls downwards, soon breaching $3.60 where our narrow stop-loss is located on the triangle edge. As long as you have a sensible bet-size, this should leave you with just a small loss on your trade, one of many that you will have to suck up as a successful trader.

The price continues to fall and triggers the wider stop-loss at $3. The price then rises again in late April to retest the breakout line at $4. Many traders, feeling pain and regret after selling at their stop-loss, would make the mistake of re-entering the trade as soon as they see the price rising back up. Those traders would soon be saddled with a second loss. If the price had actually broken upwards through the line a second time, then you would have a case to enter the trade again, but never re-enter simply out of regret. This is a recipe for disaster as you will often find yourself buying, selling, buying, selling, over and over again as the market trends sideways. I've shown a typical example in figure 19 of this type of self-destructive trading. Each up-arrow shows the opening of a trade and each down-arrow is the closing of a trade with a small loss each time. Many traders lose their entire accounts through this kind of attrition. It's death by a thousand cuts.

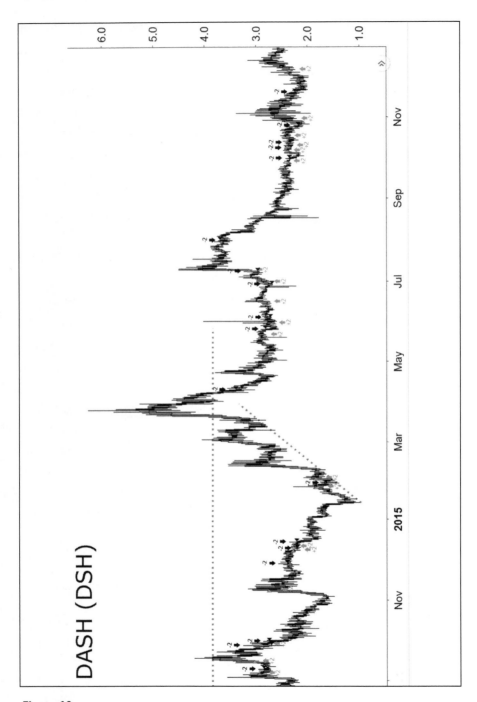

DASH (DSH)

Figure 19

Chart by TradingView

Another strategy I often employ after a sharp rise – like the one Dash experienced in March 2015 – is to take profits on part of my position and leave the rest open. For example, let's say you buy 100 DSH at $4 each during the breakout on 21 March. In less than a week, your $400 investment has become $600. You may wish to sell half of your DSH and take a profit of $100 on those 50 DSH. If you then hold the rest of the position all the way down to your stop-loss point at $3, you will take a loss of $50, leaving you with a net profit of $50 on the whole trade. It's a particularly useful strategy after a really sharp rise, because quite often a sharp rise is followed by a sharp fall, so it can make sense to hedge your bets by taking profits on a portion of your trade.

The Dash chart provides us with a common warning sign of imminent reversal. If we take a close look at the candles in figure 20, we can identify a **reversal candle**. It starts the trading day higher than the close of the previous day (the top of the candle), it then attempts to push higher, before falling again (which leaves a long top wick) and ends the day lower than the open and close of the previous day. You will find technical analysts who try to define very precisely what constitutes a reversal candle, but this is good enough for me. If the price starts off high, pushes higher and then plummets low by the end of the day, you're looking at a big flashing warning sign. And sure enough, this candle signals the start of a downtrend in DSH.

On a brighter note, when a breakout trade is going well, with the price working its way upwards, you should aim to move your stop-loss upwards to a breakeven level, so that even if the chart eventually reverses, the worst that can happen is you sell at the original buy point and end up quits.

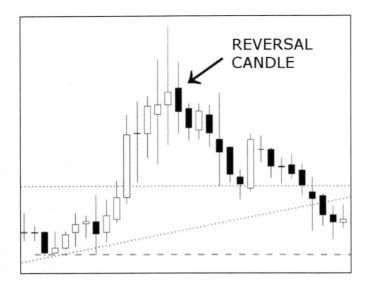

REVERSAL CANDLE

Figure 20

Chart by TradingView

SUMMARY

The question of when to sell is undoubtedly the number-one factor affecting your long-term profitability as a trader. I've shown you how to cut losses quickly on losing trades and I've also shown you techniques to help you decide where to take profits when a trend starts to bend.

If you use these techniques, you will find it a lot more difficult to join the majority of traders who lose money! Traders always obsess over which instruments to trade and exactly when they should buy, but experienced trend followers know that these are relatively minor considerations. As long as you choose to buy cryptos that appear to be heading upwards rather than downwards, the exact point of entry is not hugely important.

As you know, I like to buy on breakouts because it gives the crypto that extra oomf at the start of the trade and therefore makes it less likely that I will quickly hit my stop-loss. But this is not a key consideration. You could buy at any random point in the early stages of a trend and still make good money as long as you learn to sit patiently during an upward trend and then sell at the end in a disciplined way.

> "It never was my thinking that made the big money for me. It always was my sitting. Got that? My sitting tight! It is no trick at all to be right on the market. You always find lots of early bulls in bull markets and early bears in bear markets. I've known many men who were right at exactly the right time and began buying or selling stocks when prices were at the very level which should show the greatest profit... but they made no real money out of it. Men who can both be right and sit tight are uncommon."
>
> — JESSE LIVERMORE

Jesse understood more than anyone how difficult it is to remain in a trade that is still in a long-term upward trend but is falling short-term. Resist the temptation to constantly check your account balance to see how much more of your profit has trickled away since you last looked. Some trend-following fund managers have even admitted putting the song 'Hold On' by Wilson Phillips on repeat in the office, to try to boost their traders' morale:

> *"Don't you know things can change*
> *Things'll go your way*
> *If you hold on for one more day"*

Now you know what to buy, when to buy and when to sell. So is that it then? Are we now all set to launch you on a stellar trading career? Not quite. There's one more major factor to tackle – position sizing. The question of how much of each crypto to buy. Putting all your eggs in one basket is a surefire way of ending up with egg on your face (because you might trip over a trading obstacle and land with your head in the basket of eggs. Or the basket might become too heavy and fall, splashing egg back up into your face. Or you might… well, you get the idea). Learning the right amounts to invest in each crypto will help you make lots of profit *and* still sleep at night, safe in the knowledge that none of your crypto positions are going to bankrupt you.

CHAPTER 11: HOW MUCH TO BUY

"There are old traders and there are bold traders, but there are no old, bold traders."

— THE UNKNOWN TRADER

IT'S ALL ABOUT RISK

WHEN YOU'RE DECIDING how much of a particular crypto to buy, your question should not be: 'How much can I afford to invest?' It should be: 'How much risk should I be taking on this crypto?'

A typical trader might think, 'I've got £10,000 to invest, so I'll be sensible and *diversify* my risk by investing £1,000 in each of ten different cryptos.'

Diversification is definitely a good thing. It's generally safer to have your money in ten cryptos than in just one, but simply splitting your money equally between them is not a very good strategy.

Let's examine why by constructing an equally weighted portfolio and stress-test how it would have performed during the 2018 crash.

EQUALLY WEIGHTED PORTFOLIO

We'll go back to 1 January 2018 and buy ten popular cryptos, invest £1,000 in each one and hold them for six months to see what would have happened. (N.B. in real life, all my stops were triggered in January so I sold all my cryptos before the crash was well underway.)

I'm using these ten coins and I've listed their start-of-2018 market cap figures:

* Bitcoin – $230bn

* Ripple – $90bn

* Ethereum – $70bn

* Stellar – $7bn ("The Future of Banking")

* EOS – $5bn (a smart-contract platform; rival to Ethereum)

* Qtum – $4.5bn (combines Bitcoin and Ethereum tech)

* ZCash – $1.5bn (anonymous transactions)

* DogeCoin – $1bn

* CloakCoin – $130m (anonymous transactions)

* CannabisCoin – $23m ("Bitcoin for Cannabis Users" – yes, really)

	% PRICE CHANGE 1ST HALF 2018	LOSS FROM £1,000 INVESTMENT
Bitcoin	-53%	-£530
Ripple	-76%	-£760
Ethereum	-38%	-£380
Stellar	-46%	-£460
EOS	+6%	+£60
Qtum	-84%	-£840
ZCash	-64%	-£640
DogeCoin	-72%	-£720
CloakCoin	-88%	-£880
CannabisCoin	-92%	-£920
TOTAL LOSS	**-61%**	**-£6,070**

There are some truly horrendous losses there. My heart goes out to anyone who invested their life savings in CannabisCoin at the start of 2018 (no doubt they're self-medicating the pain away).

The problem with this approach to investing is it takes no account of the different volatilities of each cryptocurrency. Some of them tend to rise or fall by just a few percentage points per day, whereas others swing up and down wildly. A more sensible approach is to invest more money in the calmer cryptos and less in the crazy ones, in an attempt to equalise your degree of risk on each crypto investment.

RISK PARITY ALLOCATION

Now you may have been hoping that trading cryptocurrencies would be all adrenaline-fuelled wins followed by victory laps around your private estate in the Lambo, rather than learning about risk parity allocation. But don't worry, I'm only going to show you one technique, it's easy to learn and it'll make all the difference to your trading performance.

Remember average true range from chapter 10? Well, now it comes into its own. You can add it to your charts from the **Indicator** menu on TradingView charts and in most other charting apps. It tells you the average movement per day of each cryptocurrency you apply it to, and you can use this information to adjust the size of the positions you open.

For our ten-crypto portfolio above, adjusting the position sizes to take account of daily volatility gives us:

	TRADE SIZE	% PRICE CHANGE 1ST HALF 2018	LOSS FROM £1,000 INVESTMENT
Bitcoin	£1,810	-53%	-£959
Ripple	£1,018	-76%	-£774
Ethereum	£1,811	-38%	-£688
Stellar	£627	-46%	-£288
EOS	£789	+6%	+£47
Qtum	£698	-84%	-£586
ZCash	£1,358	-64%	-£869
DogeCoin	£719	-72%	-£518
CloakCoin	£627	-88%	-£552
CannabisCoin	£543	-92%	-£499
TOTAL	£10,000	-61%	-£5,686

We've still got a thumping great loss, but it's not quite as bad as before. This is because the cryptos that were the most volatile in the past and were therefore allocated the smallest investment amounts also turned out to be the cryptos that fell most dramatically during the crash. This is not a coincidence. Prices that rise the fastest also tend to fall the hardest, that's why it's so important to adjust position sizes according to volatility.

DETERMINING YOUR POSITION SIZE

When you've selected a crypto you want to buy, you can work out an appropriate position size using ATR, according to your own appetite for risk. Let's suppose you want to buy Ethereum as the price breaks out in April 2018. In figure 1, I've added a 30-day ATR line to the chart and it shows the latest ATR reading at 40, which means the price is moving by about $40 per day.

Figure 1

Chart by TradingView

Now, we'll use a hypothetical trading account size of $10,000.* We've already discussed how successful traders tend not to risk more than 0.5 to 1% of their capital on any one trade, which in this case would be 1% of 10,000 = $100. The nearest natural stop-loss level is at the previous support line at $500, as shown in figure 1. The current buy price for Ethereum is $570, so the support would be $70 away, representing 0.7% of our $10,000 capital, so that's a sensible amount as our potential loss sits between 0.5 and 1% of our capital.

If the ATR is $40 per day, then the distance to a $70 loss would be 1.75 ATR. That is a pretty standard distance for a trend trader's stop-loss so let's stick with that.

We can therefore conclude we should buy just one Ethereum coin for $570.

If we were to buy two ETH instead, for $1,140, the ATR for this entire trade would be 2 × 40 = $80. It would take less than a day of adverse price movement for us to breach the stop-loss, which

---

* I'm using dollars to save us from having to convert currencies in this example.

is only $70 away from the buy-point. Some traders operate with a tight stop-loss like this one, but bear in mind it doesn't leave much room for your crypto to move around in and you're quite likely to hit your stop loss only a day or two after buying the crypto. Such a tight stop-loss will probably eat into your profitability over time, as more of your trades will get stopped-out in the early stages.

REBALANCE THOSE CRYPTOS

In the previous chapter, I mentioned selling a chunk of my position in a crypto if it has risen a long way, to collect some profits, and leaving the rest of the position open. Once you've accumulated a portfolio of cryptos, you need to be vigilant to the possibility of your risk levels changing. Let's take a hypothetical example where you buy equal amounts of four cryptos because they all have the same price and the same ATR. But then, two of them rise fast in price while two of them fall and soon the ATRs for the ones that rose grow much larger. This is because volatility tends to grow proportionately, in line with the absolute value of a crypto (e.g. if Bitcoin moves by $100 per day when it costs $1,000 per coin, you would expect it to move by roughly $1,000 per day when it costs $10,000 per coin). So you might end up with:

	BUY PRICE	ATR	NEW PRICE	NEW ATR
BTC	$100	$10	$200	$20
ETH	$100	$10	$150	$15
EOS	$100	$10	$100	$10
XRP	$100	$10	$75	$7.50
DSH	$100	$10	$50	$5

Your account would now be way more exposed to movements in BTC than in DSH, as BTC would tend to go up or down each day by four times as many dollars as DSH.

When things get really out of whack like this, you need to think about rebalancing your portfolio. It's problematic because the need to have a balanced portfolio is in conflict with the principle of letting your profits grow on your winning cryptos until the trend finally bends.

This is partially resolved by the cut-your-losses axiom, because you would have sold those XRP and DSH positions long before they fell that far.

You might also decide to sell perhaps a third or a half of your BTC to rebalance the portfolio. You may wish to do this when you encounter a reversal candle, because it indicates the likely direction of travel will be downwards (at least in the short term). Sometimes you will encounter ambiguous situations, where you're not quite sure whether a support level is being convincingly breached or not. This uncertainty can serve as a convenient opportunity to sell a portion of a successful crypto to lock in some profit.

PYRAMIDING

The popular strategy of **pyramiding** stands in uncomfortable opposition to the principle of portfolio rebalancing. Instead it involves *adding* to your investment when it's going well. Typically, when someone is trading on margin, if the crypto goes into profit the trading platform will let you use some of the unrealised profit on your position to trade other cryptos or to increase your position in the profitable crypto.

Generally, pyramiding involves adding smaller and smaller amounts to your relatively large initial investment (hence the pyramid shape) as the price goes higher.

I've done a fair bit of pyramiding myself over the years; for example, while Bitcoin was on its long upward journey in 2016–17. The main problem is it makes it more likely you'll be shaken out of your position by price corrections along the way. It's a lot easier to 'hold on for one more day' during a correction if your buy point was far lower down the chart. If you've got a bunch of higher breakout buy points as well, the temptation to sell on a deep correction may prove too much to resist. Also, if some of your buy points are towards the end of a trend, then when the trend eventually bends, you may actually end up with a loss on some of your later buys.

And, of course, in the context of an entire portfolio it unbalances your risk instead of rebalancing it, because you're making one position larger and larger.

Despite all of this, you may sometimes find yourself – like me – strongly tempted to pyramid when a position's looking really promising. If you do it, do it cautiously.

Pyramiding can actually make more sense when you're short-selling, because as a price falls and approaches zero, it will tend to move more and more slowly. For example, it may fall from $8 to $4 in one week and then take another week to fall from $4 to $2. The proportionate drop is the same each week (50%) but the actual dollar gain on your short position is only half as big in the second week. So, in this context, pyramiding is actually in line with the principle of rebalancing, as you need to increase your position size in order to keep the profits growing at their old rate.

And speaking of short-selling…

CHAPTER 12:
SHORT SELLING

O K, I MAY have made a bit of cash on the short side from time to time, plus there was the small matter of my £3,000 to £100,000 short-selling spree during the 2008 crash. But in general, it is *much* harder to make money on the short side than on the long side and very few traders excel at it, for a couple of reasons.

First, when you're riding an uptrend, your position size gets larger and larger (which is why you sometimes have to sell some of it to rebalance your position relative to your other holdings). This can lead to really big paydays and of course trend traders rely on these big wins to pay for all those little losses.

When you go short, the opposite happens. As the price falls, your position size gets relatively smaller, as I explained in the previous chapter. As an example, let's say you have £1,000 to invest and you put the whole lot into XRP in December 2017 at $0.25. By early January 2018, the price has reached $3.00, an increase of 1,100% and so your £1,000 has grown to £12,000!

Now let's say that instead of buying you'd waited until the crash began, and then you invested your £1,000 in a short position in XRP at $3.00. By August 2018, that $3.00 price had fallen back to

$0.25 per coin, a precise reversal of our previous example. So you might expect your profit to be the same for this short trade as for the long trade, leaving you with £12,000. But sadly it doesn't work like that. Instead your £1,000 would become... £1,917. Still a nice profit, but considering we've just successfully traded a spectacular cryptocurrency collapse, I think it's a little underwhelming (see figure 1).

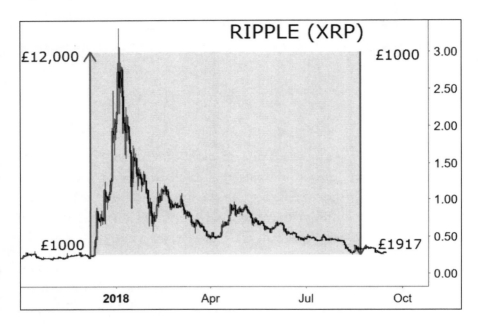

Figure 1

Chart by TradingView

As we noted, $0.25 to $3.00 is a rise of 1,100%. A decrease from $3.00 to $0.25 is a fall of 91.6%. In both cases your profit is equivalent to the *percentage change* in price, so with the long trade you make 1,100% profit, on the short trade you only make 91.6% profit. When you go short, the maximum possible gain is only 100% (if XRP fell to zero), while the maximum possible loss is *infinite* (because there is no top limit to XRP's potential price rise). Now you can see why I'm not particularly keen on shorting!

It is also much harder to stay in a short trade for weeks or months than in a long trade because the upward corrections during a downtrend can be breathtakingly sharp.

If, in figure 2, we set a rule to buy XRP when there's a major breakout and a rule to trigger our stop-loss only if the daily candle (not the wick) goes below the breakout line, then we would buy in the middle of December and hold until the change of trend in January, pocketing a handsome profit for our efforts.

If we try the same technique on the short side in January onwards, we get the result shown in Figure 2.

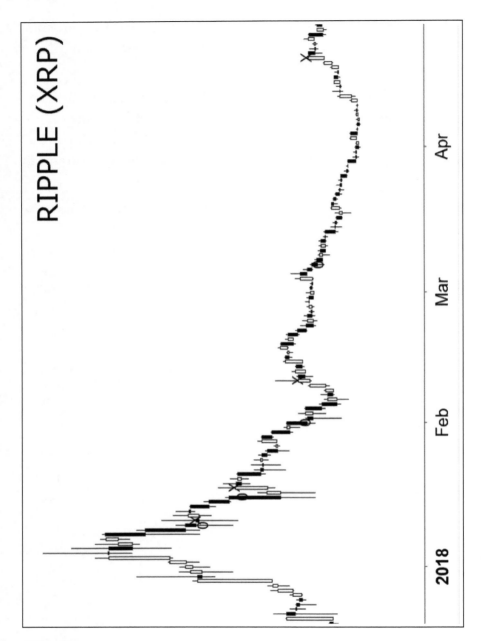

RIPPLE (XRP)

Figure 2

Chart by TradingView

Each 'o' on the chart is a short-sell on a breakout, and each 'x' is the closing of that trade when a candle ends the day back above the breakout point. Every single short trade ends in a loss, even though XRP is in a downtrend!

So clearly trading using breakouts (or break*downs*) is a non-starter because the upward corrections are too extreme. If you're still determined to give it a go, a better strategy would be to use moving averages to find a good sell point. In figure 3 I've used an **MA crossover system** with a 10-day MA and a 20-day MA. We go short ('o') each time the 10-day MA (light grey line) crosses below the 20-day MA (dark grey line), and close the trade ('x') each time the light grey line crosses back above the dark grey line.

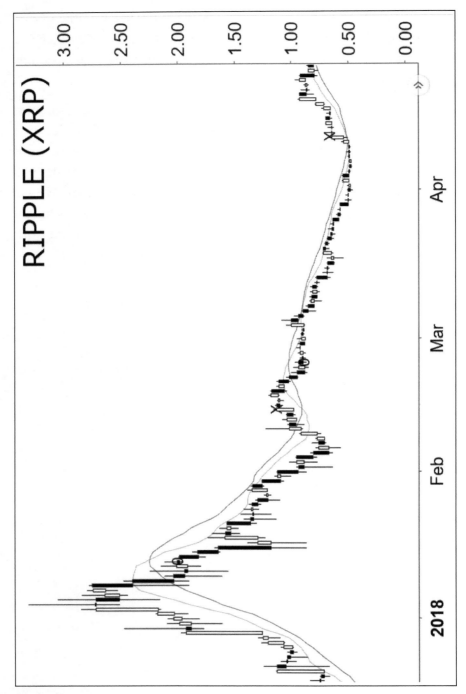

Figure 3

Chart by TradingView

This time the results are much better, there are only two short-sells and the system makes a decent profit. It should be noted, though, that this is quite a lucky trade, as the MA crossover in January just happens to take place during an upward bounce, so the next price move is downward, preventing the short trade from being stopped out.

Short-selling is obviously well-suited to a bear market but is exceptionally hard to succeed at during a bull market because the market acts like a magnet, pulling everything upwards, even the 'shitcoins'.* However, it can serve a useful function even during a bull market, by allowing you to hedge your bets and reduce the overall risk level for your portfolio.

Let's say you buy three really promising cryptos and short three shitcoins during the 2017 boom. Then you hold all your positions during the ensuing crash (bad idea). Your results might look something like this:

	OCT 2017–JAN 2018 % PROFIT	FEB–JUL 2018 % PROFIT
GoodCoin	+50%	-60%
BetterCoin	+100%	-55%
BestCoin	+200%	-65%
ShitCoin	-20%	+80%
ShitterCoin	-10%	+85%
ShittestCoin	-5%	+90%

During the boom period, you make big profits on your three long trades and smallish losses on your three short trades, because even the shitcoins are being dragged upwards by the boom. During the crash period, you lose a lot of money on your long trades but make a lot more on your short trades. Obviously this strategy only works if you correctly identify beforehand which are the truly shit coins,

---

* A 'shitcoin' is the cryptocurrency industry term for crap projects with no future. E.g. "I've got major fomo, dude. The whales are even ramping shitcoins now. They're lambo'd up and I'm eating spam."

the ones likely to rise the least in the bull market and fall the hardest in the bear market.

ISN'T SHORT-SELLING A BIT EVIL?

'Think positive', 'a positive approach', 'positive growth'. We're always taught to see the word *positive* in a positive way (unless an athlete has tested positive for crack cocaine). Likewise, we're expected to show our positivity about shares or cryptocurrencies by buying them. Nobody ever writes books about 'The Power of Negative Thinking', do they?* The problem with short-selling is it sounds awfully negative. It involves deciding a cryptocurrency is a bit rubbish and its price is going to go down, so you're going to sell it short and give it a bit of an extra shove down the staircase.

When the banking crisis took hold in 2008 and I was shorting bank shares, the media painted my kind as the true villains of the tale. *"Robbers in pinstripes"* one newspaper called us (which was totally unfair as I favour a polka dot ensemble with sequin-trimmed brocade). Financial regulators claimed we were forcing down the prices of banking shares and turning perfectly healthy banks into basket cases. Of course, that was not what was happening at all, but every financial panic needs a scapegoat for the authorities to blame.

These banks were all basically insolvent, they had huge debts and in a world where governments didn't bail them out with taxpayers' money, many of them would have simply gone bust.

Short-sellers actually *help* with the process of putting a fair price on a business. They root out lies, fraud and balance-sheet manipulation when 'positive' traders are too busy being cheerleaders to look carefully at the figures. They help to sober up overexcited markets with a healthy dose of reality.

---

* Except for this one: www.amazon.co.uk/Power-Negative-Thinking-Unconventional-Achieving/dp/1477807241

Ten years on, nobody's blaming the short-sellers for the financial crash anymore. We now know it was the bankers, the regulators, the mortgage brokers, the credit ratings agencies, but at the time the authorities chose an easy target. In their minds, the short-sellers were just being a massive downer and if only they would stop being so negative, banking shares would recover, and that would somehow magically make all the banks solvent again, and we'd all live happily ever after.

In September 2008, the UK regulator banned any new short-selling of banking shares (sadly for the regulator, it was too late to affect me, my short trades were already off and running months earlier).

A few days later, the US followed suit, with the chairman of the Securities and Exchange Commission declaring, "the emergency order temporarily banning short selling of financial stocks will restore equilibrium to markets."*

Hoorah! At last, we will have market 'equilibrium'. Let's check out that much-ballyhooed equilibrium in figure 4.

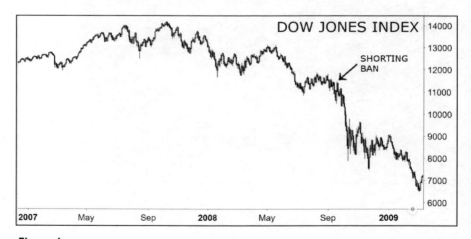

Figure 4

Chart by TradingView

---

* 'S.E.C. Temporarily Blocks Short Sales of Financial Stocks', *New York Times*, 19 September 2008. www.nytimes.com/2008/09/20/business/20sec.html

What? That wasn't supposed to happen!

The shorting ban made little if any difference to the downward path of financial stocks. Banking shares continued to fall because they were pure junk and hardly anybody wanted to buy them anymore. Unfortunately, they dragged the rest of the stock market – and the world economy – down with them.

As we discussed earlier, the heroes of the book and film *The Big Short* were short-sellers who spotted the banking problems earlier than everybody else. They didn't keep this knowledge quiet, they told anyone who'd listen! They wanted to save the world before it was too late, but nobody was interested in hearing their negativity.

Simon Cawkwell, Britain's best known short-seller, has embraced his notoriety and revels in the nickname Evil Knievil. When I met him, he seemed more like a jolly Santa (with a sack stuffed full of bad news.) He even signed my copy of his book.

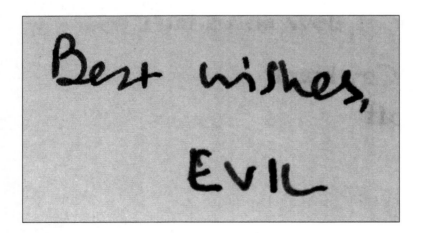

PART 3:
PUTTING IT ALL TOGETHER

"The game does not change and neither does human nature"

— JESSE LIVERMORE

CHAPTER 13: THE MISSING ELEMENT

S O YOU'VE OPENED your trading account, you've learned the proven rules in this book, many of which traders have been using to generate huge profits for centuries. You set to work and after a year of hard graft you sit back to review your progress.

You've lost all your money.

What? How is this possible?

Even though you learned the rules and really tried to follow them, you were led by what felt like an irresistible force to make irrational decisions time and time again.

The missing element is the human one.

THE TRAGEDY OF JESSE

Jesse Livermore is my hero, as you've probably gathered from the frequent quotations. His insights were a revelation to me and many other successful traders. I highly recommend the book *Reminiscences of a Stock Operator* by Edwin Lefèvre.* Based on detailed interviews

---

* www.harriman-house.com/reminiscences

with Jesse himself, it's as close to an autobiography as you'll get and contains all his finest trading wisdom.

But Jesse didn't know about **position sizing**. Such ideas were not yet widely known in the trading community. My rules about risking small percentages of capital on each trade would have seemed alien to him. Jesse used to bet huge, which is how, as a teenager trading in the 'bucket shops' of Boston, he acquired the nickname Boy Plunger. It's also how he went from being penniless to being one of the richest people in the world, to being penniless again, to being one of the richest again, to being penniless, etc.

His roller coaster career took a great toll on him mentally and on 28 November 1940 he walked into the cloakroom of the Sherry-Netherland Hotel in Manhattan and shot himself. In his suicide note, he told his wife: "I am a failure... I am tired of fighting."

It breaks my heart to hear him say those things. If he'd had access to modern money management rules and psychological insights, I sincerely doubt he would have come to such a tragic end.

I've already talked you through the risk management side of things which will help to prevent you from going broke like Jesse and will protect you from some of the extreme ups and downs that can break a person's spirit.

In the next chapter, I will explain the psychological flaws or **biases** we all suffer from, and how they tend to affect our trading performance. Being aware of your own flaws and weaknesses will make all the difference between success and frustrating failure. The rest will be up to you. I can program rules but I can't program you.*

---

* Note to self: For *The Crypto Trader* 50th Anniversary Edition, replace sentence with "I can program rules and I can also program you. Please upload your brain at glengoodman.com. Results guaranteed."

CHAPTER 14: WHERE'S YOUR HEAD AT?

O NE MORNING IN the mid-2000s, I got out of bed, had breakfast, travelled to work, and as I approached the ITN building I saw a colleague smoking a ciggie outside. He was staring at me with a worried look on his face.

"Are you alright, Glen?" he asked. "You look like a zombie!"

I stared at him blankly.

"I just lost £12,000 trading," I replied and walked into the office.

By this point in my life, I had already accumulated most of the knowledge I've passed on to you in previous chapters. I was a seasoned trader with a shelf-ful of books in my head and financial success under my belt. But that was precisely the problem. After years of learning to deal with failure, I was being sabotaged by success.

Learning how to trade is only half the battle. The other half is in your own head.

MARGIN CALLS

Most people *hate* losing money and traders are no different. We find the pain of losing £1,000 far greater than the pleasure from gaining £1,000. This imbalance can sometimes skew our trading decisions in unprofitable ways but it's also a useful natural instinct that protects us from destitution.

For years, my trading capital was protected by my cautious instincts until I started making good money trading. And the more money I made, the more risk I took, because the thing about profit is it's not *real* money is it? It's play money, it's gambling money, it's doesn't-really-matter-if-I-lose-it money, because it wasn't really mine in the first place.

That sums up how I felt, until the day I lost £12,000 and trudged, zombie-like, to work, utterly traumatised by my own stupidity. It wasn't a life-changing sum to lose. To be honest it didn't really affect my overall finances, but I just couldn't believe I'd made such a rookie mistake. It shook my whole idea of myself as a self-possessed, competent trader.

I'd made a lot of profit in the weeks leading up to this screw-up – around £12,000 profit, in fact; how's that for not-a-coincidence? I saw a trading opportunity on the FTSE 100 – it was breaking out, it was going up, I was convinced of it – so I put on a sensibly sized trade. Sure enough, the market continued to rise. I was feeling overconfident.

Hang on, I thought, it's crazy to have so little money riding on this when I *know* it's going to continue upwards. My spread-betting account, though still small, was bulging with profits, people at ITN often asked me for advice as a trading expert, and I was starting to feel I was an unstoppable money maker. I was sure the market was going up so I doubled my stake. As if by magic, the market turned on its heel and started heading downwards. This is OK, this is fine,

I thought to myself, just a normal correction in an upward trend, exactly as one would expect, I just need to sit tight.

Soon I was starting to sweat slightly as the FTSE 100 refused to recover as it so obviously should. It triggered my stop-loss and I was out, with a frustratingly large loss (because I had doubled my stake). And of course the moment I sold, it started climbing again!

So I had been right all along. I bought back in, and also I had that big loss to make up for now, so I impetuously put on four times my original stake. I was going to win big time. Definitely.

Up it went! So I bought even more. This would be my greatest victory yet.

Four hours later, I was staring feverishly at the screen. I couldn't take my eyes off it. I needed to pee so badly but there was no time for that. The market had fallen back below my stop-loss, but I'd overruled it. Bloody stop-loss, thinks it's so clever, well I know better. This market's going back up!

Soon I was getting emergency margin calls from my broker. Because I was spread betting on leverage, I had eaten through all the money in my account and if I didn't immediately deposit more, my position would be automatically closed by the broker. So out came the debit card and another few thousand went into the account.

Two hours later, I had to whip out the debit card again.

Another two hours later, the FTSE wouldn't stop falling, my current account was cleaned out and it would take days to transfer money from my savings account. This was the end of the line. Through a mist of tears and frustration, I had to close the trade. I had lost £12,000 in one day.

TOTALLY MENTAL ACCOUNTING

Fifteen years earlier, economist Richard Thaler worked out why I was going to lose £12,000 in 15 years' time. He developed the theory of **mental accounting**, yielding numerous insights about how we behave irrationally with money. His experiments showed gamblers didn't treat 'house money' they had recently won at a casino in the same way they treated money they had earned through working. They were far more reckless in their gambles with house money.*

Likewise, I was reckless and arrogant because I had 'won' a lot of money trading. Never mind the fact that it had taken weeks of painstaking effort to win that money, it still felt like a windfall and so I took a risk I would not usually have taken with money I earned through my day job.

Thaler also identified a second cause of my little disaster, a desperation to break even. Because my first FTSE trade went wrong, I became more willing to take on excessive risk in an effort to make up my losses, even transferring money from my bank account.

So there are two crucial lessons here:

1. NEVER CHASE LOSSES.

2. WINNINGS ARE REAL MONEY, NOT GAMBLING CHIPS.

In chapter 15, we'll gather together all the lessons we've learned into one almighty world-beating formula. And speaking of lessons…

---

* Thaler and Johnson, 1990. 'Gambling With the House Money and Trying to Break Even: The Effects of Prior Outcomes on Risky Choice'. www.researchgate.net/publication/227344939/download

DESTRUCTIVE DISPOSITION

In chapter 3, I introduced two key rules:

1. GROW YOUR PROFITS

2. CUT YOUR LOSSES

These are the most important rules of all and are the hardest to follow because they go against our basic instincts to avoid pain and seek pleasure. We love the pleasure of selling winners and we hate the pain of selling losers and making the loss 'real' so we avoid it.

The disposition to sell winners too early and ride losers too long was first identified in the aptly titled 'The Disposition to Sell Winners Too Early and Ride Losers Too Long' by Professors Shefrin and Statman (1985).[*] They called this human tendency the **disposition effect**.

In 1997, UC Berkeley Assistant Professor Terrance Odean brought out a brilliant paper analysing the broker accounts of 10,000 traders over a six year period.[†] He found a strong disposition effect at work and suggested it may account for the significance of "reference points", or what we call support and resistance levels, as demonstrated in figure 1.

---

[*]   Shefrin and Statman, 1985. 'The Disposition to Sell Winners Too Early and Ride Losers Too Long: Theory and Evidence'. www.researchgate.net/publication/4743153_ The_Disposition_to_Sell_Winners_Too_Early_and_Ride_Losers_Too_Long

[†]   Odean, 1998. 'Are Investors Reluctant to Realize Their Losses?' faculty.haas. berkeley.edu/odean/papers%20current%20oversions/areinvestorsreluctant.pdf

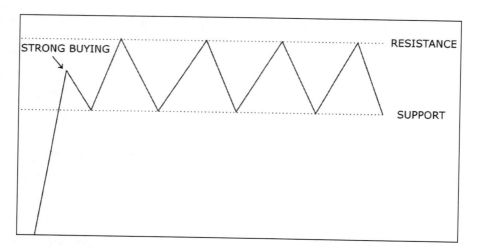

Figure 1

Odean's theory says if a lot of traders buy at a particular level, and the price then starts falling, most of them will be reluctant to sell and realise a loss, so selling pressure eases and the price starts rising again. If the price then rises above the buy point, some traders will be more willing to sell to realise their profit, and this selling pressure will tend to push the price down again.

So we can see how the disposition effect can create support and resistance levels around the point where lots of people have bought.

Most illuminating of all his findings is that in the year after these 10,000 traders sold their winning stocks, those sold stocks went on to gain 3.4% *more* than the losing stocks the traders were still clinging onto. The losing stocks continued to underperform the rest of the market rather than bouncing back in the way the traders clearly hoped they would.

Glen's handy tip: diversification really helps me cope with having to cut losses. Each of my positions is small as a proportion of my total portfolio, so when one doesn't work out, my loss is never more than a drop in the ocean and that makes it feel easier to ditch the loser.

SINKING, SINKING, SUNK

Imagine you've booked a skiing weekend in Switzerland for £500 which you're really looking forward to. A few weeks later you book another skiing weekend, in France, this time costing £1,000. Even though France costs more, you think you will enjoy the Switzerland trip more than the France trip.

Suddenly you realise you've accidentally booked them both for the same weekend and there are no refunds! You must use one ticket and waste the other. Which ski trip will you choose?

- £1,000 trip to France
- £500 trip to Switzerland

Sixty-one students were asked this question for a psychological study[*] and most of them said they'd choose the France trip because they'd spent more money on it.

If you chose the France trip like the psychology students, you've fallen for the **sunk-cost fallacy**. The rational choice would have been to go on the Switzerland trip because you believed it would give you more pleasure than the France trip, but your judgement was swayed by the costs you'd already incurred (or sunk). The fact is, those sums of money were gone, spent, no longer relevant. An AI program would have not allowed the spent money to affect its decision, which should be made purely on the basis of which holiday would give the most satisfaction (assuming the AI program could find a pair of skis to fit a desktop PC).

---

[*] Arkes and Blumer, 1985. 'The Psychology of Sunk Cost'. pdfs.semanticscholar. org/e456/4b88ca2349962a707b76be4c75076ad6bd43.pdf

In chapter 3, I described how I held onto Gameplay shares until they were worth virtually nothing. This was an example of the sunk-cost fallacy. I had put a lot of time and effort into researching the company, even visiting their headquarters. I'd also put a lot of money into the stock and I couldn't bear the idea of not getting a good return – so I was willing to hold on and lose even more money, in the forlorn hope of one day getting paid back for my trouble.

The rational course of action would have been to write off the lost money as a sunk cost and move on, but instead I threw good money after bad.

Why do we hold on to a dying investment, when at least part of our brain knows we'll probably lose even more money in the long run? It's because – as a lot of research shows – we don't care as much about 'future us' as we do about 'present us'. We are generally prepared to accept more pain in the future rather than accept less pain now.

These days, when I sell a stock or a crypto, I consciously move on immediately. I don't usually check that crypto's price performance over the coming days and weeks, and think about what could have been, I just forget about it and move on to greener pastures.

If you chose the France trip, you can console yourself with the fact that clever people make this mistake all the time. As I write, the British government is pressing ahead with the huge HS2 railway scheme, despite the fact the public is against it, most politicians are against it and it could end up costing far more than expected... but £4bn has already been spent on planning, before any track has even been laid. That would go to waste if the plan was scrapped. The money's spent, it's gone, so that shouldn't really factor in the decision, but politicians are emotional human beings and therefore the £4bn *does* matter to them. So they'll carry on regardless – current estimate £55bn, with leaked reports suggesting this could rise to £80bn, or higher...

LOSSES CAN BE FUN!

Losses can be fun! Well, OK, maybe not fun, but a good way to make yourself feel better about taking a loss on the chin is to think about the lovely tax-loss you're taking. Firstly, if you're making enough profit to be eligible for Capital Gains Tax, congratulations! Second, if you're feeling bad about selling at a loss, just think about how it will help to reduce your tax bill.

In the UK, crypto traders' profits are currently taxed in a similar way to profits on shares. In other words, if you're an ordinary retail investor, you'll probably pay capital gains tax on any profits (net of losses) once you've used up your tax-free allowance (which is £12,000 for the 2019/20 tax year).*

If you experience a string of losing trades, it can really start to get you down, but try tossing a coin hundreds of times. As I mentioned earlier, you'll soon find you get regular streaks of five heads in a row or seven tails in a row. Losing streaks are inevitable in trading, and they don't mean you're a bad trader, but if the losses start messing with your head, then you might start self-sabotaging and that's the last thing you want.

Also, there's a possibility that you've entered a genuinely difficult trading environment. Some months (or years) it's easier to make money because markets are trending nicely, other months not so much.

So take it easy on yourself. If you experience a string of losses, consider scaling down your trade sizes for a while so it doesn't hurt so much each time.

---

* Very large and sophisticated investors may be classed as 'conducting a trade' and according to HMRC they would pay income tax and national insurance on their trading profits instead of capital gains tax, but HMRC stress that this would only be in 'exceptional circumstances.' In addition, profits from cryptocurrency mining or crypto payments received from an employer would also be income, rather than capital gains. All this could change, of course, so check the HMRC website for the latest guidance.

YOUR CRYPTO IS NOT YOUR BABY

There's a whole cupboard-full of psychological biases related to getting over-attached to trades. 'The endowment effect', 'status-quo bias', 'familiarity bias', 'confirmation bias' and more. They all attempt to explain our tendency to treat our possessions with an extra-special fondness. That was yet another mistake I made with Gameplay – I became emotionally attached to the company and to my investment.

Investing/trading is about making money. It is not about making a new coin-shaped friend or having a special plaything to take care of. Bitcoin investors have shown themselves to be particularly susceptible to these attachment biases. The whole HODL phenomenon has drawn thousands if not millions of people into a quasi-religious belief in Bitcoin's destiny as the ruler of all currencies. It's basically the millennial equivalent of the baby-boomer 'goldbug' phenomenon. Goldbugs are (usually quite wrinkly) people with an obsessive belief in the unassailable worth of the yellow metal, which they hold in large quantities regardless of whether its price is rising or dropping like a stone. Some of these people held most of their savings in gold between 1980 and 2007, a period of 27 years where gold's price rose by precisely 0%.

If you question these people's belief in the supremacy of their special magic rock, they get very defensive indeed. So don't bother arguing with them, believe me, it's not worth it – just back away slowly.

The main psychological bias HODLers suffer from is **confirmation bias**, the tendency to seek out information that confirms their existing beliefs and to ignore information that contradicts or questions them. If you really want to build up a case that Bitcoin will destroy all other currencies, I'm sure you'll find enough information online to fill a hundred ring-binders (printing out and filing information is a particular favourite of goldbugs, as it makes your case look pretty solid if it fills an entire bookshelf). The problem is, if you were so inclined, you could find an equal amount of information making the opposite case. I recommend trying to remain dispassionate about investments and keeping an open mind.

Long-term HODLers also fail to take account of the **opportunity cost** of HODLing. This economic concept is about all the alternatives you miss out on when you make a particular decision. If you hold most of your savings in gold for 27 years and it makes you no profit, this isn't a neutral outcome, it's a highly negative outcome, because those same savings could have been earning a ton of profit for you in the stock market. Your opportunity cost is all the profit you've missed out on.

I've explained previously in this book why HODLing through bear markets is not a great idea. Well, HODLing through long sideways markets is also not a great idea, because of the opportunity cost involved.

If you find yourself stuck in an investment that's going nowhere, try playing devil's advocate by pretending you don't already own the crypto, and then ask yourself whether you'd be interested in buying it. If the answer's 'no', then you need to think about whether you should still be holding onto this crypto.

EVERYBODY'S TALKING ABOUT IT

People tend to invest in cryptos they've heard about and they tend to give undue weight to the most recent bits of news they've heard. Psychologists call the first instinct the **herding bias** and the second the **availability heuristic**. It obviously feels more comfortable to trade well-known cryptos like Bitcoin than obscure ones, but that's not always where the big money is made.

Cast your net wide, check out some of those cryptos on your trading platform whose prices are starting to perk up, even if you've never heard of them before. I've made plenty of real-life-cash from investments that mean virtually nothing to me and nobody's talking about.

Who cares? Profits are profits. I'm not fussed about whether I buy my next car with my Bitcoin winnings or my ObscureCoin gains.

I GOT A HOT TIP!

There is no phrase in the world more likely to precede financial disaster than 'I got a hot tip'. I've tried extremely hard to resist the lure of these tips over the years but I have occasionally given in to temptation and *always* regretted it. Tips may come from trusted family members, your most intelligent friend, the wealthiest pundit on CNBC, but wherever they come from you must **ignore them at all costs**. I suggest recalling the immortal wisdom of legendary screenwriter William Goldman:

> "Nobody knows anything… Not one person in the entire motion picture field knows for a certainty what's going to work. Every time out it's a guess and, if you're lucky, an educated one."[*]

What goes for the movie industry goes double for trading. Never forget – NOBODY KNOWS ANYTHING about the future.

IT'S AN ABSOLUTE BARGAIN

> ***CON-MAN-COIN NOW ON *SALE*** Price slashed for one day only!!! RRP $2. ~~Was $1.50. Was $1.~~ Now reduced to $0.50 per coin for this limited period!! Do not miss!!!

Few of us can resist a bargain, which is why we easily fall into the classic trading error of trying to **catch a falling knife** – which means buying an asset after a sudden drop, assuming it to have

---

[*]   *Adventures in the Screen Trade* by William Goldman.

dropped as low as things can go (only to discover otherwise with the loss of your fingers). And yes, that was yet *another* mistake I made with my Gameplay shares, buying even more shares after they'd fallen in price because they'd become *such* a bargain.

A lot of people made the same mistake with Bitcoin and other cryptocurrencies after the peak of the 2017 boom. **Anchoring bias** causes us to normalise certain price levels and accept them as the true, natural price levels.

We've already seen how support and resistance levels are often created by people anchoring their expectations and feelings to certain price levels (usually the price they originally paid for an investment). A lot of people also fixate on the highest price an asset has recently reached and think of it as the right price, which of course means any lower price must therefore be a bargain.

Ripple (XRP) suddenly became enormously popular in December 2017 and its price rose by more than ten times in less than a month! As you can see from the volume bars in figure 2, a lot of the buying took place near the top of the chart and many of those buyers will have anchored their price expectations firmly to those heady levels. As the price started falling, they will naturally have felt this new lower price was a bargain and then an even lower price was seen as even more of a bargain, etc., and many will have have kept buying more XRP all the way down. (I know a few people who did exactly that.)

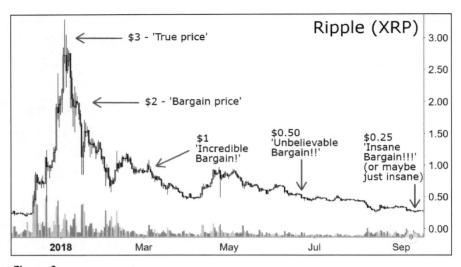

Figure 2

Chart by TradingView

Figure 2 demonstrates the essence of catching a falling knife. Buyers of XRP at $2 will have bloodied themselves as that knife continued to fall through their fingers and will have caught a few more gashes at $1 and $0.50.

Once again, don't listen to the argument that you haven't really lost any money if you don't sell your cryptos. It's meaningless. If you're holding onto a ton of XRP you bought at $3 and it's now worth $0.25 then that is a real loss of real money. If you don't believe me, go to a crypto forum and ask someone if they'll swap your 25 cent XRP for $3 in fiat currency.

I'M ONLY HUMAN AFTER ALL, DON'T PUT THE BLAME ON ME

Only last night I slept terribly because I was full of regret at a breakout I'd failed to notice in time. I'd gone off to a TV news studio to be interviewed about cryptocurrency, so I missed a breakout in

XRP, and now my FOMO was off the charts. Did I get out of bed and buy that crypto anyway in order to cure my FOMO? No sir, I did not. I sucked up that FOMO and stuck to my trading plan. Chasing missed breakouts is the road to ruin.

Instead I waited patiently (albeit in a bad mood) for the next good setup to establish itself. Just a day later there was another breakout and this time I bought at the right time, the price took off like a rocket at the breakout and I made a nice 50% profit on that trade.

We're all soft and squishy human beings with bad moods and short attention spans. It's OK to have irrational feelings about trading, it is not OK to knowingly act out those feelings with your trading account.

Understanding all the psychological biases in this chapter will not cure you of them, but it will make you more aware of when you are suffering from one of them and that awareness will allow you to choose not to let those biases dictate your trading decisions. Know yourself, then make money. In that order.

CHAPTER 15: ESCAPING THE DAILY GRIND

D EAR READER, WHEN it comes to rushing about, I am a bit of a lazy git. I really hate getting up early and working in a stressed environment. In my mid-20s I was lucky enough to be given my own daily show on LBC radio. Unluckily, it was at 5–6am, so it ruined my social life and I eventually quit, to become a TV news reporter at the BBC and at ITV.

I was on the news every day, it was stimulating and challenging, people would regularly recognise me in the street and say how much they liked my reports. But it still involved getting up early, squashing my nose into someone's armpit on a packed London Tube commute and then rushing around for nine hours in a mad panic to put together a report in time for the evening news.

By 2012, I was making more money each year from investing than I was from my day job. It was nice to have two incomes, but I felt it would be far nicer to have just one investment income and a cosy duvet. So I quit. I basically semi-retired in my 30s and I've never been so happy.

I get up when I feel like it, do a fair bit of pottering about in my pants, and spend plenty of time (but not too much) with my family.

I can while away the hours in this way simply because I've chosen to examine daily price charts, not minute-by-minute charts. My trades are relatively few and far between, and as explained earlier, this is actually a far more profitable way to trade than sitting glued to a screen all day. If you day trade you will probably lose money in the long term. Statistical fact.

THE GOOD(MAN) LIFE

The chart setups I like tend to take weeks or sometimes even months to form. When I've got my eye on a crypto, I add it to my **watchlist**. TradingView or pretty much any other charting app will allow you to keep your own watchlist.

You can simply check your watchlist each day (or a few times a day) to see if any action's taken place, but obviously you'll occasionally miss a breakout if you're only checking from time to time. Alternatively, you can set **price alerts** that send you a text message whenever particular price levels are breached.

If you don't want to miss even the first moments of a breakout, then you can place stop orders in the market, so that you automatically buy (or sell) a crypto when the breakout begins. The only problem with this approach is that you will encounter a lot of frustrating false breakouts, where the price quickly spikes upwards and then back down below the breakout level. Sometimes this all happens in mere seconds and you'll find yourself making a lot of small losses. Setting alerts means you can quickly check out the chart before deciding when to enter the trade.

What you *shouldn't* do is stare at the trading screen all day, waiting for something to happen. This will cause you to get itchy trading fingers. As your brain gets bored and searches around for things to do, you'll start seeing opportunities where there are none and entering into trades with a low probability of success. So not only will you be wasting time staring at screens, but it will make you poorer into the bargain. Why not take your mind off the markets by reading a good book instead? Or write a book (hey look, that's what I've just done).

ADDING CRYPTO TO YOUR PORTFOLIO

If you already trade shares, commodities, forex, or perhaps all of that and more, then adding cryptocurrency into the mix could enhance your overall performance.

Aside from the sometimes spectacular returns in the crypto market, there is the key benefit of **non-correlation**.

If, for example, you only trade UK shares, then you have massive exposure to a single market. If it crashes badly, you lose a lot of real money very quickly. If you diversify by investing in US shares as well, then you have lessened your exposure to the UK, which is a good thing. If the US economy booms and the UK economy goes into recession, then you may find your US shares rise while your UK shares sink, so your portfolio should be less volatile than if you were in just one market.

The problem is the US and UK stock markets are *strongly correlated* – in other words, they tend to move together in the same direction a lot of the time. When one crashes, the other tends to crash too. In order to lower the overall risk of your portfolio, you need to invest in markets that are *not* strongly correlated with the stock markets, so that profits in one market may counteract losses in another market.

So far, all the data shows only weak correlations between cryptocurrency movements and share prices, government bonds or the price of gold. When stocks fall, cryptocurrencies are usually unaffected. This is great news for investors as it suggests adding cryptocurrencies to your portfolio should lead to a reduction in overall risk (or higher returns for the same level of risk.)*

FOLLOW THE RULES

It's time to put it all together now. Here's a quick reminder of some of the main lessons in this book:

- grow your profits
- cut your losses
- trade the trend until it bends
- keep your trade sizes small enough to sleep at night
- do your research on a crypto and read the white paper
- don't fall in love with your crypto
- diversify and spread your risk
- keep your charting clear and simple
- winnings are *real* money, not gambling chips
- never chase missed breakouts
- never chase losses by throwing good money after bad
- never try to catch a falling knife
- run away from tips, rumours and opinions
- control your inner voices and psychological biases
- avoid scams; if it sounds too good to be true, it usually is.

---

* Chuen, Guo, Wang, 2017. 'Cryptocurrency: A New Investment Opportunity?'. papers.ssrn.com/sol3/papers.cfm?abstract_id=2994097

CHAPTER 16:
AND FINALLY...

I N MY EARLY years as a TV reporter, I was the guy they'd call on to do the 'And finally...' stories. If there was a dog who could bark "sausages" or a ghost spotted on the A406, you could guarantee I'd be there. I was beaten up by a four-year-old Kung Fu master, I danced with the cast of *The Lord of the Rings*, I tried to snog the veteran pop group Bananarama (which they handled pretty well).

What I didn't do was check my trading charts, mid-snog. There was no option to do that on the road in the pre-smartphone era. And that was frankly liberating. It meant I had to place all my stop-orders in the evenings. Trading was my after-hours hobby that just happened to be earning me more and more money.

Of course, placing orders that triggered in my absence was not 'optimal'. Sometimes I'd get home and see I already had a loss on a trade that had opened automatically that morning, because it had been a false breakout. Sometimes I'd find a profitable trade had automatically been closed when a stop-loss was triggered, only for the price to bounce straight up again.

The reality is these **whipsaws** are inevitable, whether you're sitting at the screen or not. They're an acceptable cost of trend-trading, acceptable because a few big trends pay for all those little losses. And also acceptable, because they mean you can be a successful trader and still have a full life away from the screen.

A new generation has woken up to trading because of the invention of cryptocurrency, and they now have a chance to free their money from the fund-management bloodsuckers, and get wealthy in their spare time, as I did.

I sincerely hope this book sends you on your way to that prosperous future, and please feel free to get in touch using the details below as you make your journey. I'm ready to answer any questions you may have about what you've read. Bye then.

Website: www.glengoodman.com

Facebook: www.facebook.com/thesharesguy

Twitter: @glengoodman

TradingView: GlenGoodman

INDEX

A

altcoins 32

Amazon 26, 29–30

American Express 29

amount to buy 195–202

anchoring bias 229

ask price 80

attachment bias 226

Augur 34

availability heuristic 227

average true range 174–6, 184, 198–200

B

basing pattern 109

bear market 98, 126, 151, 193, 209–10, 227

bell curve 179

biases 93–4, 216, 226–7, 229, 231, 235

bid price 80

big round numbers 97

Big Short, The 52, 54, 212

big swinging dicks 46

Binance 72–3, 82

Bitcoin 7–11, 159–60

   blockchains 28–9

blocks 28
Buffett opinion on 26
cost of mining 148
crashes 19–23, 43, 51, 94, 109, 144, 148, 229
creation of 26–8
day trading 85–6
fundamentals 135–6
how to buy 70–5
lack of middleman 29–31
mining 28–9
offshoots of 32
in portfolio 196, 198, 200–1
as reserve currency 9
scammers 12–14, 18
social sentiment indicator 149–50
trading curve 48–50
trends 99–101, 109–11, 114–15, 122–7, 172–3, 176–8, 184–6
whales 23
when to sell *see* selling cryptocurrencies
Bitcoin address 66–7
Bitconnect 14–17
Bitstamp 70
blockchains 28–9, 67, 136, 157
blocks 28
breakout point 110–15, 117, 125, 127, 131, 155, 158, 161–2, 164–5,
   169, 171, 184, 188–9, 193, 198, 202, 207, 230–1, 233, 235
bubble
   Internet 29–30
   stages in 24, 86–90
Buffett, Warren 26, 42, 57
bull market 23, 51, 98, 101, 115, 122, 126, 151, 158, 161, 166, 187,
   193, 209–10
Buterin, Vitalik 15, 32–3, 136

C

candlesticks 106–8, 126, 184, 191–2, 207

CannabisCoin 196–8

Capital Gains Tax 225

catching falling knives 228–30, 235

Cawkwell, Simon 212

central banks 9, 26–7, 210

chandelier stop 175

charting 104–31, 134, 136, 152, 187–8, 233, 235

Clan, The 46–51

classical charting 102–3

CloakCoin 196, 198

closed trading 16

Coinbase 70–1
  Coinbase Pro 73

Coinmama 70

coinmarketcap.com 15–17

cold wallets 68–9

compounding 57

confirmation bias 93–4, 226

continuation patterns 117–18

control the voices 95

corrections 50–1

cost of production model 147–8

Cotton, Gerald 63

crowdfunding 30

crypto exchanges 71–5, 82

cryptocurrency *see also* Bitcoin; *individual currencies*
  adding to portfolio 234–5
  Buffett opinion on 26
  definition of 9
  how much to buy 195–202
  how to buy and sell 61–83

lack of middleman 29–31
mining 29
when to sell 24, 169–94
CryptoKitties 34–5
Cryptolab Capital 147
cut your losses 44–5, 50, 55, 94–5, 187–92, 221, 235

D

Da Hongfei 157
daily line chart 107
DApps 33–4
Dash 32, 117–18, 187–8, 191
day trading 84–6
disposition effect 221–2
Dogecoin 32, 196, 198
dotcom crash 37, 180

E

efficient market hypothesis 91
E-gold 8
emotions 23, 48, 124, 179, 224, 231
EOS 43, 196, 198
Ethereum 9, 15, 33, 42–3, 76–7, 121–2, 128–31, 142, 158, 160–7,
   196, 198–9
Etherisc 34

F

Facebook 10, 12–13, 96–7, 176, 187

falling knives, catching 228–30, 235

false breakout 112, 164

Fama, Eugene 91–2

Fear, Uncertainty and Doubt *see* FUD

Fear Of Missing Out *see* FOMO

fees 81, 85

fiat currencies 28, 62, 70

Financial Services Compensation Scheme 82

Finatext 149

flags 118–19, 130–1, 162, 186

flash crashes 155

FOMO 11–13, 20, 92–3, 112, 231

forks 32

FTSE 100 218–20

FUD 20–1

fundamentals 132–53

G

gambling 19, 218, 220

Gameplay 36–9, 45, 48, 50, 224, 226, 229

GitHub 135–6

global financial crisis 26–7, 51–2, 181–2, 195–8, 203, 210–12

goldbugs 226–7

Goldman, William 228

Golem 34

Google 26, 29–30

Google Chrome 41

Graham, Benjamin 132

grow your profits 50, 55, 95, 221, 235

H

Hayes, Adam 148
head, where's yours at? 217–31
head-and-shoulders pattern 119–23, 125, 181
herding bias 227
high-frequency trading 85
HODL 21–5, 40–3, 226–7
Hold On for Dear Life *see* HODL
Homma, Munehisa 106
hot tips 228
hot wallets 63–8
Howells, James 67–8

I

ICOs 10, 136–42, 151
Indicators 105, 197
Instagram 10
interest rate 83
Internet Explorer 41, 43

J

Jeffries, Daniel 157

K

Kahneman, Daniel 92
Kaminska, Izabella 8
Kennedy, Joseph 2
Keynes, John Maynard 53
Kraken 73–81

L

Ledger Nano S 69
Lefèvre, Edwin 213–14
leveraged trading 75, 78, 82–3
Lewis, Martin 12–13
Lewis, Michael 52
limit order 78
liquidity 71–2, 80
Litecoin 32
Livermore, Jesse 84–5, 94, 99, 183, 187, 193, 213–14
LocalBitcoins 70
log charts 176–7
log-periodic power law 179
losing trades 38–40, 44–5, 192 *see also* cut your losses

M

MA crossover system 207
margin trading *see* leveraged trading
MarketPsych 150
MasterCard 29, 70
Matos, Carlos 14–15, 17
memes 11, 20, 39–40
mental accounting 220
Metaverse 101
Metcalfe's law 145–7
Microsoft 41
mining Bitcoins 28–9
mining cryptocurrencies 29 *see also* mining Bitcoins
MoneySavingExpert.com 12–13
moving average crossover 173
moving averages 99–100, 170–6, 184

Mt. Gox 8
Mycelium 64–8

N

Nakamoto, Satoshi 26–8, 148
NEO 157–9
Netscape 41, 43
network effects 55
network value to Metcalfe *see* NVM ratio
network value to transactions ratio *see* NVT ratio
news blackout 151–3
Newsweek 28
non-correlation 234
Northern Rock 51–2
NVM ratio 145–7
NVT ratio 142–5, 147

O

Odean, Terrance 221–2
offline/cold wallets 68–9
One Coin 14
opportunity cost 227
order book 79–81

P

PayPal 29
PCs 30, 33–4, 102
Performance of Technical Trading Rules 45
phishing 142
Pipster 149

Ponzi, Charles 13–14
Ponzi schemes 13–18
portfolio 195–202, 209, 222, 234–5
position size 198–200, 203, 216
positions tab 79
price alerts 233
price chart 75
price–earnings ratio 143
private key 62–3, 68–9
pyramiding 201–2

Q

Qtum 196, 198
QuadrigaCX 63

R

random walk theory 92
Reddit 22
Reminiscences of a Stock Operator 213–14
reserve currency 9, 31
resistance line 109–10, 164–5, 171, 188, 222, 229
reversal candle 191–2, 201
right-angled triangle 114–15, 131, 162–3, 165–6
Ripple 42, 89–90, 156–7, 196, 198, 204, 206–9, 229–30
risk parity allocation 197–8
road map 140
Rodrigue, Jean-Paul 23–4, 87
roller coaster meme 20

S

S&P 500 180–3

Santiment 127–8, 154–5

scammers 12–13

   Ponzi schemes 13–18

Schabacker, Richard W. 102–3, 118

Securities and Exchange Commission 211

selling cryptocurrencies 24, 169–94

Shiller, Robert 92

short selling 52–3, 122, 203–12

Sinclair, Clive 133–4

Sinclair C5 133–4

smartphones 30

social sentiment indicator 143, 149–51

spread 80, 85

spread betting 82–3, 159–60, 219

Stellar 196, 198

stop order 78, 112

stop-loss 112, 171–2, 187–9, 191, 193, 199–200, 219

stopped out 115

sunk-cost fallacy 222–4

support line 109, 222, 229

symmetrical triangles 116–17, 161–2, 164, 185–6

T

target, choosing 96–103

tax 82, 159, 225

taxi companies 31–2

Technical Analysis and Stock Market Profits 102

ten-bagger 50

Thaler, Richard 92–3, 220

tickers 75–7, 104

trade the trend 54–5, 91–5
trading form 77–8
trading pairs 76
trading screens 72–81, 104–31, 233–4, 237
TradingView 104–7, 109–10, 112, 118–19, 122, 128–31, 155, 158–9, 162–7, 171–4, 180–5, 188, 190, 197, 199, 204, 206, 208, 230, 233
traditional currencies 26–7
trailing stop 171–2, 175
transparency 16, 33
trend bends 86–90, 153, 169–70, 180–2, 184, 192, 201–2, 235
trend trader 88, 91–5, 170, 186, 203
trending sideways 98
Trezor Wallet 69
triangles
   right-angled 114–15, 131, 162–3, 165–6
   symmetrical 116–17, 161–2, 164, 185–6
tulipomania 2
Tversky, Amos 92

U

Uber 31

V

venture capital 30
virtual wallet 62–3, 71, 142
   hot wallets 63–8
   offline/cold wallets 68–9
Visa 29, 70
volume 75, 126–7

W

wallet address 62
Walliams, David 13
watchlist 233
wedges 117–18, 155–6, 181
whales 23
"When Lambo?" 10–11
whipsaws 236–7
white papers 140–1, 235
Wikipedia 138
Winklevoss twins 68–9
Woolworth 124
World Computer, The 33

Y

yetanotherico.com 136–41

Z

ZCash 196, 198